W9-BKB-577

PENNSYLVANIA
Off the Beaten Path

"I've traveled around this state for years, but Sara Pitzer has found places I never knew existed but now want to visit. . . . It's a guidebook, and it's recreational reading as well."
—Gilbert Love, *Pittsburgh Press*

PENNSYLVANIA
Off the Beaten Path

by **Sara Pitzer**

A Voyager Book

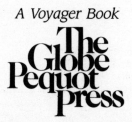

The Globe Pequot Press

Chester, Connecticut

The prices and rates listed in this guidebook were confirmed at press time. We recommend, however, that you call establishments before traveling in order to get the most up-to-date information.

© 1989 by Sara Pitzer

All rights reserved. No part of this book may be reproduced or transmitted in any form by any means, electronic or mechanical, including photocopying and recording, or by any information storage and retrieval system, except as may be expressly permitted by the 1976 Copyright Act or by the publisher. Requests for permission should be made in writing to The Globe Pequot Press, 138 West Main Street, Chester, Connecticut 06412.

Library of Congress Cataloging-in-Publication Data

Pitzer, Sara.
    Pennsylvania: off the beaten path/by Sara Pitzer.—1st ed.
       p.   cm.
    "A Voyager book."
    Includes index.
    ISBN 0–87106–622–X
    1. Pennsylvania—Description and travel—1981- —Guide-books.
I. Title.
F147.3.P57   1989
917.48'0443—dc19   88–35303
                                                      CIP

Cover illustration by Pamela Hopson
Text illustrations by Carol Drong
Composition and Maps by TRG, North Branford, Connecticut

Manufactured in the United States of America
First Edition/Second Printing

This is for Croy, with love and thanks.

Pennsylvania

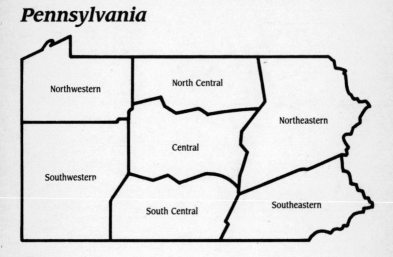

Contents

Introduction

Pennsylvania schoolchildren used to belt out a song with these lyrics:

> *Pennsylvania forever*
> *Wonderful keystone state*
> *Beautiful, rugged, glorious*
> *Fashioned sublime and great.*

They understood it. Oh sure, the part about "fashioned sublime and great" translated into "fashion sub lime and grape," which everyone supposed had something to do with a stylish variation on lemonade, probably made up in the mountains somewhere. But the rest made sense: Pennsylvania was one of the thirteen original colonies, located among those colonies in the same position an architectural keystone is in an arch—they learned that in the fifth grade unit on Pennsylvania, probably from Miss Young, who must've taught every fifth grader in the state. As for beautiful, rugged, and glorious, they saw it every day. Even in the meaner coal towns, mountains soared above the sooty sidewalks, glowing green under the sun in spring and summer, gilded with the colors of changing foliage in fall, and glinting with ice and snow in the winter. No matter where a Pennsylvania kid lived, it wasn't far to a hike in the woods or fishing in a stream or swimming in a pond. Waterfalls, rivers, and woods—these were things for a Pennsylvania kid to be proud of.

Other verses in the song praised the state's industries: lumber, iron, coal, oil, and steel. Everyone understood. That was the good honest work parents did. It was something to be proud of, too. So was farming.

And, of course, the history was special. No other state had the Declaration of Independence or the Liberty Bell. No other state had Philadelphia, Birthplace of a Nation. A kid was pretty lucky to be a Pennsylvanian.

Those lessons stuck.

As the economics of Pennsylvania changed, mining deposits ran out or demand dwindled, and major industries staggered under foreign competition, times got tough. But the waterfalls, rivers, and mountains remained beautiful, rugged, glorious, fashioned sublime and great. The history remained special. The kids became adults and reared their own kids, still knowing where to find a good place to fish or swim or hike. Still proud. They helped make and keep Pennsylvania the great place to explore that it is today.

Tourism is the second most important industry in the state today. (Manufacturing still holds first place.) By and large, it's related to the state's important history and to its magnificent geographic attributes.

Determined Pennsylvanians worked fervently, especially around the time of the American Bicentennial, on historic preservation and restoration projects. The splashiest projects are the famous ones, Independence Hall in Philadelphia; Valley Forge National Historical Park, commemorating Washington's victory over the British; and the Gettysburg National Military Park, scene of a major Civil War battle, for instance. But the projects with heart are those where citizens in smaller communities studied up on what was special about their history and set about bringing it to life, generally investing their own money and time and lots of their own sweat. For example, the people of Mifflinburg knew that their town had once produced more buggies per capita than any other town in the country. They bought and restored one of the buggy factories and now maintain the museum and take visitors through demonstration tours, all with volunteer labor. They've just burned the mortgage. In Aaronsburg, volunteers built a reproduction of an outdoor brick oven for the women of the Bicentennial Committee to demonstrate colonial baking and cooking. Such projects are the stuff of this book.

Geographically, in spite of areas of highly commercial tourism, which have their place, mind-boggling acres of forest land, as well as miles and miles of river and lakeshore, remain unspoiled because Pennsylvanians have stayed proud enough to protect it. In the northern tier, mostly wilderness, you can drive for hours, imagining that you've seen enough empty space to isolate every small warring country in the world. The rest of your life wouldn't be enough time to explore it all. Pennsylvania has 110 state parks. Only a few are described here. For a complete listing with addresses and telephone numbers, write Bureau of Travel Development, Pennsylvania Department of Commerce, 416 Forum Building, Harrisburg, PA 17120.

Other attractions change and grow. In recent years, the Amish have moved from a few areas of concentration, such as Lancaster, to farm nearly all the fertile rural areas of the state. Everyone is trying to avoid duplicating the tourist density and corresponding circus that developed around Lancaster. The Amish attractions included here are all in low-key settings, where the Amish welcome your business but desperately want to maintain their privacy.

In the past twenty or so years, wineries have flourished all over Pennsylvania. Less than two decades ago, only a few produced enough wine to sell, and even home winemakers hesitated to say in more than whispers that they produced alcohol. Prohibition wasn't so long in the past. As Pennsylvania vineyards have matured, so have the skills of the wine makers and the attitudes of the neighbors. So have the wines! More than fifty wineries throughout the state invite visitors for tours and sales. Because many of them are tiny, it is imperative that you call or write before you visit—if only to be sure someone will be available to show you around and pour a few tastes when you arrive. The larger wineries are more geared for short-notice visitors. A few of them appear in the text. The rest are listed, with addresses and, where available, telephone numbers, at the ends of several regional chapters. Just touring the little wineries in Pennsylvania could give you a vacation of several days or several weeks. And the smaller wineries are bound to produce some memorable experiences, whether you like the wine or not.

I learned about some of Pennsylvania's wilderness and natural areas from Marcia Bonta's excellent book, *Outbound Journeys in Pennsylvania,* published by Keystone Books. For longer descriptions of some natural areas and for a more complete listing of them, you might order a copy, for $12.75, by writing The Pennsylvania State University Press, University Park 16802.

With all this to do, how are you going to fit it all in? You're not—not in one seven-day trip, not even in one thirty-day trip. These experiences need to be savored, not raced through on a tight schedule. Try working a few small areas at a time, going home, and then coming back.

When you come, don't forget your map. The Pennsylvania Department of Transportation map shows the mountains and forests clearly, as well as most of the parks and natural areas. It may come to you when you write for your state park listing. If not, write Bureau of Office Services, Pennsylvania Department of Transportation, Harrisburg, PA 17120. The map of New Jersey and Pennsylvania published by the American Automobile Association shows roads clearly and identifies some small places not included on the PennDOT map.

One warning about maps and driving in Pennsylvania: Never assume that the shortest distance between two points is what it seems to be on the map, especially in the mountainous parts of the state. You have to experience it to know how winding and hilly some of those short-looking routes can be. The map just can't show what's really there. But then, that's what traveling off the beaten path is all about, isn't it?

A personal note. Although I was born in the South and live there now, I grew up in Pennsylvania, married a Pennsylvanian, and raised my children there. I traveled the back roads when they were still the main roads, working and living all over the state. Most of what I remembered as good remains; the changes, by and large, are improvements. I guess Thomas Wolfe couldn't go home again, but for me it turned into a helluva good time. I know it will for you, too.

By the way, that song ends:

> *Where ever I roam*
> *I will always say*
> *That my home*
> *Is Penn—syl—van—i—aaaaaa!*

I'm proud.

Fallingwater

Off the Beaten Path in Southwestern Pennsylvania

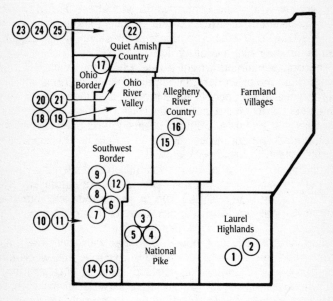

1. Fallingwater
2. Ohiopyle State Park
3. Scenery Hill
4. Always Christmas
5. Century Inn
6. Lemoyne House Historical Museum
7. Bradford House
8. Arden Trolley Museum
9. Meadowcroft Village
10. Good Intent
11. Greene County Historical Museum
12. June Stout Antiques
13. Willow Inn
14. Log Cabin Bed and Breakfast
15. Trillium Trail
16. Beechwood Farms Nature Reserve
17. McConnells Mill State Park
18. Old Economy Village
19. Royce Theatre
20. Richmond Little Red School
21. Tall Oaks Wild Animal Safari
22. Wendell August Forge
23. Amish Tour Farm
24. Cranford Inn Bed and Breakfast
25. Tavern Restaurant

Southwestern Pennsylvania

Laurel Highlands

Everyone who visits Pennsylvania should see **Fallingwater,** the famous summer retreat that the architect Frank Lloyd Wright designed for the Pittsburgh department store owner Edgar J. Kaufmann over half a century ago.

The only remaining Wright house where the original setting, furnishings, and artwork remain intact, Fallingwater has attracted more than a million people since it opened to the public in 1964, which seems to take it out of the class of hidden-away places; remarkably, it retains a feeling of seclusion and oneness with the natural environment, especially if you go during the week or in the off-season to avoid peak crowds.

The house, surrounded by rhododendron and seemingly growing out of the boulders and rock, extends over a natural waterfall and the racing water of Bull Run. A gray sandstone four-story chimney at the core of the house anchors it into the stone cliff. Architects and lay people alike know about the genius of Wright's designs, which allow the house to merge with its environment outside and to echo outdoor nature in its stone and wood interior. But touring Fallingwater, you see some of Wright's human idiosyncrasies reflected in the structure as well. For instance, tall men hunch under the low ceilings because Wright designed according to his own height—several inches less than six feet. And a guide explains that the family asked Wright's permission before making even so simple an interior change as building bookshelves in a bedroom.

Fallingwater is about two hours southeast of Pittsburgh via the Turnpike, on Route 381, between the villages of Mill Run and Ohiopyle. The house is open for tours from April through mid-November every day except Monday, 10:00 A.M. to 4:00 P.M. In January, February, and March, it is open only on weekends. A moderate admission fee is charged. For more information, write P.O. Box R, Mill Run 15464 (412–329–8501).

After visiting Fallingwater, returning quickly to busy streets and stores feels inappropriate. Stopping for a walk or a picnic along the Youghiogheny River at **Ohiopyle State Park,** just 5 miles south on Route 381, eases you back into the modern world. The park covers almost 18,500 acres. Two state game lands next to it extend the wilderness farther. The Youghiogheny Gorge, cut 1,700 feet into the Laurel Ridge by the river, takes your breath away. Should you decide to spend more time exploring the nature trails and river walks of the park or to enjoy whitewater rafting and swimming, ask about camping and boating facilities in the park (P.O. Box 105, Ohiopyle 15470, 412–329–4707).

National Pike

From the park, traveling south on Route 381 takes you quickly back to Route 40, known as the National Pike. In colonial times it was the main road connecting Washington, D.C., with points west.

About 12 miles east of Washington, Pennsylvania, the National Pike runs straight into the little town of **Scenery Hill,** where you can browse through a number of antique and specialty shops. **Always Christmas,** on the ground floor of an 1812 brick house that once housed runaway slaves, specializes in handmade Christmas tree ornaments and dolls. Call (412) 945–6242 for more information.

When you're through shopping, walk down the street to **Century Inn,** a twenty-one-room village inn that has been operating continuously since 1794. In the 1820s, Andrew Jackson and La-Fayette climbed from stagecoaches to sleep and eat here. Today, lunch and dinner are served daily (only dinner on Sundays) from mid-March to mid-December. Breakfast is served only to those who stay in one of the inn's guest rooms.

Part of the fun of visiting the inn is studying the antiques, including old kitchen tools clustered around the 7-foot fireplace. An impressive collection of antique toys and dolls fills one whole room upstairs.

The dining room serves homemade breads and a tasty assortment of near-trendy concoctions: peanut soup, brie baked with butter and almonds, and coconut cream pie, for instance.

The inn is popular, so reservations are important whether you want to spend the night or dine or both. Write Century Inn, Scenery Hill, PA 15360; phone (412) 945–6600.

Southwest Border

Downtown in Washington, visit **LeMoyne House Historical Museum,** at 49 East Maiden Street, originally the home of anti-slavery advocate Francis LeMoyne and a shelter on the underground railroad. It is open May 1 through October 31, Monday, Wednesday, Thursday, and Friday from 9:30 A.M. to 2:30 P.M., Sundays 2:00 P.M. to 4:00 P.M. Modest rates are charged. Call (412) 225–6740.

At 175 South Main Street, tour **Bradford House,** once the home of David Bradford, a leader in the Whiskey Rebellion of 1794. The home is furnished in antiques of the period and is open March 15 to December 31, Wednesday through Saturday, 11:00 A.M. to 4:00 P.M. and Sunday 1:00 P.M. to 4:00 P.M. The admission fees are modest. Call (412) 222–3604.

Continue 2 miles farther north on Main Street to Arden and the **Arden Trolley Museum.** A great treat for kids, the ride on a restored trolley car covers part of the line that once linked Pittsburgh and Washington. The museum has about twenty trolleys dating from 1894 on display and offers a tour that includes the car barn, where cars and equipment are displayed, and the shop where the old cars are restored. The gift shop, in a baggage car, sells books about railroads, as well as toys, T-shirts, and souvenirs related to trolleys. There's a shady area outside for picnicking. Hours from July 4 to Labor Day are noon to 5:00 P.M. daily; the museum is open weekends and holidays only in May, June, and September. Volunteer members of the Pennsylvania Railway Museum Association, Inc. operate the trolley museum (P.O. Box 832, Pittsburgh 15230; phone 412–734–5780).

Another great place to go with children is **Meadowcroft Village,** a bit less than 20 miles northwest of Washington, $2\frac{1}{2}$ miles west of Avella on Star Route 50. This historic site, developed by Albert and Delvin Miller, preserves the family's history of farming and breeding and racing horses. Some buildings have been brought in from other locations to recreate all the village activities. Tours include demonstrations of baking and blacksmithing and a chance to sit in an old one-room schoolhouse with a potbellied stove. The Country Kitchen serves light meals, or you can use the outside picnic tables to eat a packed lunch. Meadowcroft Village is open May 1 through October 31, Wednesday through Saturday, 10:00 A.M. to 5:00 P.M. and Sundays 1:00 P.M. to 6:00 P.M. Moderate rates are charged. Call (412) 587–3412.

If you're interested in strange little towns for their own sake, rather than for the attractions in them, travel west from Washington on Route 40, almost to the West Virginia border, to **Good Intent,** at the headwaters of Wheeling Creek's Robinson Fork. There's nothing here. Nobody knows how the village got its name, but it seems to be apt. And it seems to have started being apt almost from the beginning of the town's history. In the early 1800s, Peter Wolf built a grist mill here. The mill pond filled up with silt, so he had to start over farther downstream. They never got around to creating a main street in town. Two grist mills, two blacksmiths' shops, a tannery, a stage company, a harness and saddle shop, a post office, and a Baptist church have all come—and gone. Nobody teaches in the schoolhouse. Somebody lives in it. The general store doesn't sell anything but coal and wood stoves and it's only open on Saturday. There's more: The town doesn't have local government, but it does have an unofficial mayor, who lives somewhere else.

Folks who live here like it just the way it is. They say that along with all the things Good Intent doesn't have, it also doesn't have crime, hurry, legal contracts, or selfishness. People help each other in times of sickness. They seal agreements with nothing more than a handshake. As Don Hopey, a *Pittsburgh Press* reporter put it, "Once you make up your mind all you need is food, shelter, and companionship and realize you don't really have to keep up with the Joneses, then you can begin to enjoy life."

Providing shelter has become an almost contradictorily successful business in Good Intent for Curt and Ruth Naser, who run a log-home building business. But their success is under control; they live in a modest log home themselves.

To get there, take Road 62118 from Claysville on Route 40. Go west to Road 62120. This will take you across the Danley covered bridge into Good Intent. When you get into town, be careful not to run over the Guinea hens. Like the rest of the town, they mean well.

When you're ready to return to the world of getting and spending, if you're seriously interested in fine food and in fine antiques and like the idea of enjoying both together, plan to spend time around Waynesburg. Three miles east of town (take Exit 3 off interstate 79) the **Greene County Historical Museum,** a mid-Victorian mansion, features thirty-five rooms furnished in antiques of the periods, a country store, collections of pottery, glass, quilts, and Indian and early American artifacts. Also on the grounds are a country schoolhouse and a narrow-gauge steam locomotive. The museum is open April 1 through November 1, Tuesday to Sunday, 12:30 P.M. to 4:00 P.M. for a modest fee. Call (412) 627–3204 for information.

When you're through looking at museum antiques, you might visit **June Stout Antiques** with an eye to buying some good pieces of your own. June's antiques fill most of the rooms in her Federal-style, four-on-four brick home built in 1858, plus seven other buildings, just outside the village of Ruffcreek. June prides herself on selling no "collectibles" but only what fits her definition of true antiques—one-of-a-kind handmade pieces at least one hundred years old. Within the definition, she's got everything nameable, from books, vintage clothes, china, and silver to dining tables large enough to seat fifty. She'll show it all to you, for as long as your strength holds up, entertaining you with a running commentary on the antiques, the neighbors, her family, and anything else that comes to mind. "My son says to take a nerve pill when you come in," she says.

Inevitably, if you stop at June's, you'll go through the kitchen, where you can't miss her huge parrot, which spends its time alternately sitting atop (and outside) its cage and riding on the back of one of the cats. Somewhere in the house you'll come across the sign her son gave her: THIS IS NOT A MUSEUM. THIS JUNK'S FOR SALE.

"Anything I have bought is for sale," June says, meaning that she doesn't indulge in the habit of some antique dealers of keeping the best pieces she finds for herself. However, if it was given to her as a gift, you probably can't buy it at any price. People call June from all over the country for help in locating hard-to-find pieces. She welcomes business in the shop, but she isn't always home, so while she'll let you in almost any time if she knows you're coming, you definitely should make an appointment before you go. Call (412) 627–6885. To get there, take Exit 4 off Interstate 79 to Ruffcreek, then go $1/2$ mile north on Route 221.

June says you can see many of the antiques she's found at **Willow Inn,** 6 miles south of Waynesburg in the village of Oak

Forest. Willow Inn is an authentically restored 1790 home, furnished mostly in original painted furniture dating from the early 1800s.

Ralph Wilson, who does all the cooking at the inn, restored it himself. The other proprietor, Patrick Verner, who waits on the tables, got frustrated back in 1975 that he couldn't find the kind of primitive paintings he wanted for the inn, so he decided to paint some himself. Guests buy these pictures of village scenes, groups of animals looking slightly pie-eyed, and frolicking children almost faster than Pat can paint them.

Willow Inn offers no printed menu; dinner, which is whatever Ralph decides to offer that night, costs $35 a person; lunch is $27. Meals are served seven days a week by reservation at least forty-eight hours in advance. It's worth the money and the planning. Ralph's seven-course meals are imaginative and delicious, plentiful, and not the least bit pretentious. Everything you taste invites pause to figure out all the flavors. Ralph grew up cooking, always trying to produce something unusual from ordinary ingredients. According to Pat, an uncle of Ralph's once said, "Can't Ralph cook a plain egg?" Apparently he can't, but he makes a mean tomato dumpling soup, wonderful whole wheat bread, lovely veal with green peppercorns, incredible carrots and strawberries Amaretto, amazing walnut bourbon torte . . . ah, Weight Watchers, alert! Write Willow Inn at R.D. #4, Oak Forest Road, Waynesburg, PA 15370 or call (412) 627–9151. Pay by cash or check; no credit cards are accepted. To get there, take Route 18 south out of Waynesburg 3 miles to the village of East View. About 1/2 mile south of East View, take a left on the Oak Forest Road. Go 3 miles to the village of Oak Forest. Willow Inn is the first farm on the right past Oak Forest.

The better part of wisdom warns against driving far after a meal like that. Pat and Ralph recommend staying at **Log Cabin Bed and Breakfast,** just 6 miles down the road. Jane and Terry Cole welcome you into a restored 1820 colonial log home with three huge guest rooms, furnished with family antiques to be "not fancy, just comfortable," as Jane puts it. The original log cabins themselves are unchanged, though a colonist come to life probably would be surprised by the modern baths and Finnish sauna, even if the Coles' coffee by the fire or lemonade on the porch seemed familiar. Rates include continental breakfast. Payment is by cash or check, no credit cards, and reservations are required (412–451–8521).

Allegheny River Country

Just northeast of Pittsburgh off Route 28 are several special outdoor nature spots. In early May, visiting **Trillium Trail** delights wild-flower enthusiasts. Following an easy $1/2$-mile trail reveals countless thousands of white trilliums blooming on the hillside above a ravine, where in addition, many labeled wild flowers along the way catch your attention every few steps. You won't be alone here during bloom season, but part of the fun is seeing how many different sorts of people enjoy an unspoiled show of wild flowers. This is a good place to go with children, because the undemanding trail takes a relatively short time to walk. From Route 28, take the Fox Chapel Road exit and drive nearly a mile to Squaw Run Road. Turn left. A mile down the road you will come to a fork in the road. Both choices lead to parking lots for the trail.

Nearby, **Beechwood Farms Nature Reserve,** which, like Fallingwater, is a property of the Western Pennsylvania Conservancy, has longer and more varied trails. Run by the Audubon Society, the reserve is great for wild flowers, birds, and photography. As suggested by the names of some of the trails, "Goldenrod Trail" and "Violet Trail," spring is a good time to stop here, too. The trails are open from sunup to sundown.

Just before you pick up Goldenrod Trail, you can watch a wind generator in action; farther down the trail Canadian geese populate a pond. As you follow the trails on into the woods, you'll see many different birds.

The Evans Nature Center in the reserve includes a book and gift shop and nature displays, as well as a group of truly enthusiastic volunteers, who keep everything running smoothly. They provide you with maps, information, and advice on where to walk depending on your particular interests. The reserve is open Tuesday through Saturday, 9:00 A.M. to 5:00 P.M. and Sunday from 1:00 P.M. to 5:00 P.M. To get to the reserve, take the Fox Chapel Road Exit north from Pa. Route 28. Go nearly a mile. Turn left on Squaw Run Road. Drive just over a mile. Take a left fork to Dorseyville Road. Beechwood Farms is almost 2 miles down the road on the left.

For more information about the reserve write 614 Dorseyville Road, Pittsburgh 15238; phone (412) 963–6100.

Ohio Border

More directly north of Pittsburgh, you'll find **McConnells Mill State Park,** which has something to appeal to history buffs, geologists, birders, botanists, rock climbers, hunters and fishermen, rafters, and, of course, picnickers. The feature from which the park gets its name is a restored grist mill. A covered bridge dating from 1874 just below the mill is still in use. To get to the mill and bridge, you have to park in a lot near the top of the hill and follow a foot path down. You may take a free guided tour of the mill in the summer or go through on your own.

While you're in the mill, pick up a brochure and a map for the Kildoo nature trail, a 2-mile loop, not as easy as the walks at Trillium Trail and the Beechwood Farms Nature Reserve, but unusual in that a paved area at the beginning of the trail accommodates people confined to wheelchairs. Along the trail, depending on the season, you'll see a variety of evergreens, wild flowers and lichens, and many species of ferns. Also in the park, you can study the geological wonders of Slippery Rock Gorge, some 20,000 years old and 400 feet deep, and other rock formations that have been there millions of years. For more information about tours, hunting, and fishing, phone (412) 368–8091. To get there, it's easiest to take Interstate 79 40 miles north from Pittsburgh to the Route 422 exit. Go almost 2 miles west on Route 422. A sign indicates a left turn for the park.

Ohio River Valley

You can appreciate some more recent history on a trip to **Old Economy Village,** at Ambridge, less than an hour northwest of Pittsburgh. Old Economy is a preserved village of the old Harmony Society, which was founded in this country when the society's leader, George Rapp, brought a group of his followers from Germany to avoid persecution and live in the promised land.

The Harmonites believed that the second coming of Christ was about to happen. They became a communal, celibate society so they would be pure when it did.

Rapp's first settlement, which he called the "First Terrestrial Home," was Harmony, Pennsylvania. The Harmonites turned out to be good makers of cloth as well as craftsmen and farmers, and they produced impressive profits in manufacturing. They established their "Second Terrestrial Home" in Harmony, Indiana, because they needed more land and wanted to be close to a navigable river and western markets. Nobody knows why the group moved again in 1824, but they came back to Pennsylvania to build Economy, 20 miles north of Pittsburgh on the Ohio River, where they quickly established themselves as a successful manufacturing community.

Their beliefs did not suggest that being ready for the New Kingdom meant that they had to give up the niceties of this one. They practiced the Divine Economy, a melding of their religious principles, economic ideas, and social life. Religion came first in their lives, but their communal lifestyle was not austere. Harmonites ate well, made and drank wine, adorned their furniture, wore silk on Sunday, played music, planted flower gardens, and made money for the community.

The eventual demise of the society in 1905 happened for several reasons. The followers of George Rapp expected him to lead them into the New Kingdom, so when he died in 1847 without that having happened, the faith of many was seriously shaken. Also, about a third of the society's members had left during an earlier rift. Finally, any celibate group that stops taking in new members and can't give birth to its own obviously lives on borrowed time.

Although when they ran out of members, their social and religious experiment ultimately stopped working, their canny business sense produced fine furniture, sturdy buildings, beautiful grounds, and many beneficial investments in the nearby towns. It's fascinating to reflect on all this as you tour the village.

You should allow at least half a day for your visit. Not only is the formal tour long (it can take well over an hour), but also you'll want to allow time to look around some more on your own and to browse in the gift shop and gardens. The tour includes the community kitchen, the cabinet and blacksmith shops, the gra-

nary, wine cellar, tailor shop, store, great house, and other buildings. You have a lot to see and a lot to think about here.

Tour guides know much about both the religious beliefs and
the history of the community. When an old object has been
placed somewhere it was not originally placed or when restoration somehow deviates from the original structure, the guides will
point it out and explain. The guides do an outstanding job of
answering questions.

The village is open Tuesday through Saturday from 9:00 A.M. to
4:00 P.M. and Sunday from noon to 4:00 P.M. (closed Mondays and
holidays, except Memorial Day, July 4, and Labor Day). Moderate
rates are charged. For information about daily tours and special
events, write Harmonie Associates, Fourteenth and Church
Streets, Ambridge 15003 or call (412) 266–1803. To get there, exit
Interstate 79 at Coraopolis and take Route 65 along the Ohio
River to Ambridge.

Within about a 30-mile radius of Ambridge, each of several
communities has a special attraction worth stopping to see. If
you continue north on Route 65 you come quickly to Rochester,
where Frank E. Davis operates the **Royce Theatre** in the Frank.
E. Davis Studios, a theatrical supply company specializing in sets
and lighting. The Royce Theatre is Frank's long-time personal
passion, a miniature composite of the great movie palaces of the
thirties, scaled 1 inch to 1 foot. It's a complete theater in miniature, operating exactly as a full scale theater did in the golden
years of movies. It has a stage, a regular screen and a Cinema-
Scope screen, a pit orchestra and a stage orchestra, and a pipe
organ—all to scale. The pit orchestra and the organ are on miniature elevators that raise them to stage level at performance time.

Frank Davis has assembled a library of classic films, especially
musicals, as well as the appropriate newsreels and cartoons of
the time, to show with all the orchestra and organ preliminaries
typical of the thirties. You could, for instance, see *Fan of the Op-
era,* or *Can-Can,* or the newsreel of the Lindbergh kidnapping
story, preceded by a Bugs Bunny cartoon, all showcased by music
from the Tommy Dorsey Orchestra.

In the story behind the scale theater (where audience members
sit in full-sized seats, happily), Frank's father and his grandfather
were theater people before him, so Frank's earliest experiences
were in the grand old theaters. At home he amused himself by

11

copying the sets. His first model, built from a cardboard box, he lit with Christmas tree lights he had asked his grandmother to give him for Christmas. The Royce Theatre culminates about sixty years of theatrical and modeling activity. Today at 75 Frank loves running shows for visitors. "It seems like such a waste to run it just for myself," he said.

Your visit includes an organ prologue, newsreel, cartoon, coming attractions, and main attraction. Open by appointment only. The address is 630 New York Avenue, Rochester 15074 and the telephone number is (412) 774–2133. A moderate admission fee is charged.

A few minutes north of Rochester, still on Route 65, New Brighton offers another kind of individual enterprise, the Lapic Winery Ltd, operated by Dennis and Josephine Lapic. The winery is open daily for wine tasting and sales except election days and major holidays. Family tours are held on Sundays. The tours include the vineyards as well as the winery, and group tours also include a slide show in the Old Wine Cellar and complimentary wine tasting. Call ahead (412–846–2031) to arrange tours, or write 682 Tulip Drive, New Brighton 15066.

A poke and a plum away (poke your head out the car window and you're plum outta town), Beaver, on Route 68 between Routes 51 and 60 has **Richmond Little Red School,** a one-room schoolhouse used from 1844 until 1950, now restored with many of its original furnishings. A group of local volunteers, some of whom received the first eight years of their elementary education in the red brick school, got together to put it back into shape. They act as hosts and guides to visitors, answering questions about what it was like to go to school there.

The original bell hangs in place over the door, the pump out front has been painted red to match the brick, and the "functioning" outhouse (not exactly the same as the original, but a genuine outhouse, nonetheless) does what outhouses have always done. Because the building gets cold in winter and heats slowly once a fire is built in the potbellied stove, the volunteers prefer not to schedule group tours in the dead of winter. The school is open Sundays from 2:00 P.M. to 5:00 P.M. in June, July, and August. Tours may be arranged by appointment. Write Park Road, Beaver 15009 or call (412) 775–1989.

Another stop that seems especially suited to children is **Tall Oaks Wild Animal Safari,** just off Route 168 in Ohioville Boro,

Darlington. Animals roam freely on a thirty-five-acre compound; visitors sit in a tractor-pulled wagon with seats, driven through the acreage by a guide who can help identify unfamiliar animals. You'll find about 150 different animals on display, though the number is always growing. Look for buffalo, elk, Sicilian donkeys, ostriches, emus, rheas, pigmy goats, sheep, peacocks, and fallow deer. A petting zoo at the end of the tour gives children a chance for some hands-on experience with animals.

Tall Oaks is open approximately May 1 to October 31, depending on the weather, every day from 10:00 A.M. to 5:00 P.M. and weekends only after Labor Day. Rates are moderate.

From all these little towns you can get to a surprisingly pleasant and scenic section of Interstate 76 if you want to proceed quickly to points north or south for more exploring.

Quiet Amish Country

When you drive between Erie and Pittsburgh, the urge is nearly irresistible just to get on Interstate 79 and stay there, unless you have some specific reason to get off. This stretch of Interstate 79 is entirely rural, scenic, fairly lightly traveled and more pleasant than most interstate trips. But roughly halfway between Erie and Pittsburgh, it's worth taking some time to go both east and west on Route 208. The easterly road goes into Grove City (a pretty little college town), where you can visit **Wendell August Forge.** Grove City is close to where Interstates 80 and 79 intersect. From Interstate 79, take Exit 31 or from Interstate 80, take Exit 3A. Both are clearly marked with signs directing you into Grove City; more signs lead you directly to Wendell August Forge at 620 Madison Avenue. It's like finding a tiny self-contained industry in the middle of a quiet community where everyone else is doing something else. This is one of the few remaining forges in the country that still makes forged aluminum, pewter, bronze, and sterling silver pieces by hand, without any production machinery.

The forge was founded in 1923 by, predictably enough, Mr. Wendell August, who discovered that light metals could be made decorative by forging rather than casting them. Originally, the forge produced ornamental gates, grills, tables, and the like, mainly for larger institutional buildings. At the end of each job, Mr. August would present the customer with a small bowl or vase from the forge. These gifts turned out to be so popular that the entrepreneurial Mr. August began producing gift items for sale.

Today the forge is operated by another entrepreneurial businessman, Bill Knecht, who decided to leave the IBM corporate life to run his own business in a small town and in 1978 bought the forge. A team of thirty-five master craftsmen now produce aluminum, bronze, pewter, copper, and sterling silver pieces. A die cutter creates the original die, and then the pieces are hand hammered from the dies. The hammered pieces are colored over the forge fire and then hand finished. No two pieces are ever alike. Visitors are allowed to walk through the shop section of the forge to see the entire process in action and ask the craftsmen questions. You can also watch the award-winning master glass engraver, Gene Scala, at work as he uses tiny stone wheels to engrave elaborate designs in crystal.

In the showroom, all the items produced at the forge are for sale for prices ranging from a few dollars to a few thousand. Plant tours for individuals are available Monday through Saturday, 8:00 A.M. to 4:00 P.M.; the showroom is open Monday through Saturday, 8:00 A.M. to 5:00 P.M., Friday until 9:00 P.M., and Sunday 11:00 A.M. to 5:00 P.M. The phone number at the forge is (412) 458–8360.

Going west on Route 208 from Interstate 79 takes you to Volant, about 10 miles away from Grove City, and 4 miles farther, New Wilmington, the charming, historic home of Westminster College. This is the heart of a refreshingly noncommercial Amish area as well.

The Amish Tour Farm offers you an opportunity to learn about the religion, culture, and customs of the Amish without gawking offensively or intruding on their privacy. The 150-acre farm originally belonged to Levi Hostetler and his family. In 1983 he decided to sell the farm and move to Ithaca, New York, to join a stricter community. James Winner, not of the Amish, bought the property and with great attention to authenticity turned it into a tour facility to show how the Amish live. No Amish people are involved with the project, although they have cooperated in providing detailed information to help keep the tour accurate. Inside, the home is furnished much as Hostetler had it, with simple furniture pushed back against the walls and no rugs on the floors except the throws the Amish make themselves. Guides dress in costumes similar to the clothing the Amish wear, but each costume has some element about it that is deliberately "incorrect" so that they will not seem to be pretending to be Amish. All this is carefully explained to visitors.

The tour includes a short film about the Amish, followed by an information period during which guides offer more information on Amish history and their life-cycle events, from birth to death. Guides are thoroughly versed and spend a lot of time answering all questions, even the often asked, "What kind of underwear do they wear?" For that information the staff went directly to the local Amish community.

The final part of the tour takes in the barn and barnyard, buggy shed, outbuildings, fields, and animals. All the farm equipment is the old John Deere machinery used by Amish farmers in the area.

The people of the tour farm work hard not to offend the sensitivities of the local Amish; no one wants to see the carnival atmosphere that has taken over Lancaster duplicated here. Visitors are asked not to take photographs, as the Amish do not believe in being photographed. They believe it is against the biblical injunction against making graven images to one's self. The sign identifying the tour farm is very small, so that it is difficult to distinguish it from the neighboring working farms, in keeping with the Amish saying, "Self-praise stinks." If you want to see this Amish countryside and learn about their lives here, it is important that you go prepared to observe the same courtesies. Tours are available from 10:00 A.M. to 4:00 P.M. Tuesday through Saturday and noon to 4:00 P.M. Sunday. The tour farm is on Bend Road, R.D., New Wilmington. Call (412) 962–2992 or 962–3535.

Just a few miles away, in Volant, **Cranford Inn Bed and Breakfast,** run by Donna and Morris Green, offers lodging and breakfast to travelers, by reservation. The Greens had lived in the huge old house for some time before they decided to strip it down, restore it, and turn it into a bed-and-breakfast inn. Donna says, "It's not exactly colonial and it's not exactly Victorian. It's 1900s everything." The antiques, milk glass, china, and old photos in the inn are all family pieces, the legacy of parents who never threw away anything. One of the inn's three guest rooms is done in Amish style and features a canopy bed made by a local Amish craftsman. Guests who stay here are treated to coffee and tea in their rooms to wake up before breakfast. Rates are modest. Write Mercer Street, Volant 16156; call (412) 533–4497.

The perfect place for lunch or dinner, if you stay at Cranford Inn, is the **Tavern Restaurant** on State Route 208 in New

Wilmington. Although white farm buildings of the Amish dominate the countryside of New Wilmington now, the area originally belonged to the Lenape Indians, one of six nations of the Iroquois. The Delaware and Seneca tribes took the land away from the Lenapes; later the settlers took it away from the Indians. Sometimes today old farmers whose families don't want the rural life feel that now the Amish are taking the land away from them. To get back to the Tavern, a frame building dating from the early 1800s, the town doctor lived here originally, and the house was part of the underground railroad during the Civil War. In more recent history, the Tavern has fed many generations of students and faculty from Westminster College (coeducational since its founding in 1852) with uncompromisingly high quality traditional foods and an atmosphere of understated elegance. Two of the downstairs dining rooms have fireplaces. The Tavern is especially famous for its chicken dishes and stuffed pork chops. One recipe involves coating chicken pieces in egg and flour, browning them lightly, then baking them inside a covered pan with steam sealed in. Prices are moderate. The restaurant is open daily noon to 2:00 P.M. for lunch and 5:00 P.M. to 8:00 P.M. for dinner and Sundays noon to 6:30 P.M.; it is closed on Tuesdays from July 4 to Christmas. Many people come here for sentimental visits and special occasions, so it is important to make reservations. Call (412) 946–2020.

Off the Beaten Path in Northwestern Pennsylvania

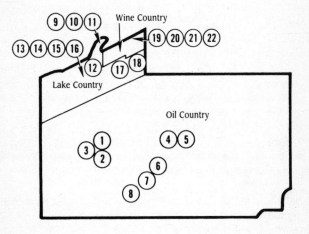

1. Allegheny College
2. Market House
3. Baldwin-Reynolds House
4. Drake Well Park and Museum
5. Pithole Ghost Town
6. Oil Creek and Titusville Railroad
7. Oil Country Inn
8. Debence Antique Music Museum
9. Presque Isle State Park
10. Nature Center
11. Ecological Reservation
12. Gull Point Sanctuary
13. East Boat Livery
14. Flagship Niagara
15. Firefighters Historical Museum
16. Erie Historical Museum and Planetarium
17. Waterfall Restaurant
18. Shades Beach Township Park
19. Freeport Public Beach
20. Brown's Village Inn
21. Hornby School Museum
22. Lake Shore Railway Museum

Northwestern Pennsylvania

Oil Country

In the northwest part of the state, tucked away in small towns along the way, several places are interesting enough to lure you from the ease of the interstate. Just off Interstate 79, in Meadville, where the zipper, originally called the "hookless fastener," was invented and first produced, **Allegheny College,** one of the oldest colleges west of the Alleghenies, has a good collection of Lincoln memorabilia in the Pelletier Library. Ida Tarbell, one of the first muckrakers, donated the materials, acquired when she wrote an early, extensive biography of Lincoln, to her alma mater. Tarbell was one of the college's first female students. She majored in biology because she hoped that with what she could learn through a microscope she could find God. She remained a devoted alumna till she died. The library also has many interesting papers, books, and artifacts related to Miss Tarbell. Two of the college buildings, Bentley Hall and Ruter Hall, are listed on the National Register of Historic Places.

Meadville's historic downtown includes more than a dozen historic buildings that should interest those who care about old architecture. A self-guided tour to historic points in Meadville is available wherever tourist literature is distributed; better yet, pick up the tour brochure at **Market House,** 910 Market Street. This is the commercial and cultural center of the community. The Crawford County Tourist Association office is on the second floor. On the ground floor, a farmers market flourishes, as it has for over 100 years. You can pick up a bite to eat at the lunch counter there to hold you over while you shop through the array of produce, flowers, baked goods, handcrafts, cheese, ceramics, and collectibles in the marketplace. Market House is open year-round, Tuesday, Thursday, Friday, and Saturday, 7:00 A.M. to 3:30 P.M.

One of the homes on the self-guided tour of the Meadville historic district, the **Baldwin-Reynolds House,** 639 Terrace Street, is open to visitors. It was built in the early 1840s for U.S. Supreme Court Justice Henry Baldwin and remained in the family until it was taken over by the Crawford County Historical Society.

It is furnished in period antiques and also includes tools, textiles, glassware, and clothing of the period. It is next to a country doctor's office of the 1800s. From Memorial Day through Labor Day, tours are offered Wednesday, Saturday, and Sunday, 1:00 P.M. to 5:00 P.M. The last tour begins at 3:30 P.M., and the rates are modest. Call (814) 724–6080 for further details.

Approximately 30 miles east of Meadville, you can get a fascinating glimpse of the early influence of oil, before Texas or foreign countries even thought of it, in Pennsylvania. Start at Titusville with the **Drake Well Park and Museum,** the site where the *world's* first successful oil well was drilled. The well is topped by a replica of the derrick. The museum contains a detailed history of the early oil days, including a twenty-five-minute film about how the first well came to be drilled. In the library are thousands of photographs from the early oil days. The library also holds more papers of Ida Tarbell, in this case those related to her famous exposé, *The History of the Standard Oil Company.* Her own family had been involved in the beginnings of the oil industry, and this background pushed her away from science into journalism, writing about oil. Her personal scrapbooks, including clippings of some of her reviews, bring the story down to a personal level quite different from the accounts of history books.

The park is ¹/₂ mile southeast of Titusville on Route 8. The museum (814–827–2797) is open from 9:00 A.M. to 5:00 P.M., Tuesday through Saturday and noon to 5:00 P.M. Sunday. A modest fee is charged.

A short drive southeast on Route 27 and then south on Route 227 brings you to Plummer, about 1¹/₂ miles farther south from which you'll find the ghost town of **Pithole.** It was an oil boom town in the late 1860s and was abandoned when the oil business fell off. A museum building on the grounds contains a pictorial history of Pithole and artifacts of the area, but by far the most interesting activity here is wandering across the site of the town, where nothing remains but cellar holes, wells, and the depressions of streets. It's a little as it might feel to go to a Texas oil town and find nothing left but grassy mounds of earth where people and businesses used to thrive. You can pick up a walking tour brochure at the visitor center, open from Memorial Day to Labor Day, Wednesday through Sunday, 9:00 A.M. to 5:00 P.M. Modest fees are charged to visitors. Call (814) 589–7912 for information.

19

One interesting way to learn what happened in this area during the rise and decline of the oil industry is to make the tour by car with the Oil Country Auto Tape Tour, a do-it-yourself tour of Oil Creek Valley from Titusville to Oil City, with fifteen historic points noted along the way, including Pithole and Petroleum Center. Rent the tape and a cassette player either at the Drake Well or at the Holiday Inn in Oil City, then return it at the other end of the tour. For details phone (814) 827–2797.

There are several other ways to see some of the oil country and historic sites while enjoying a respite from highway driving. One is to ride the **Oil Creek and Titusville Railroad,** sponsored by the Oil Creek Railway Historical Society. The trip, which takes two hours, runs from Titusville to Rynd Farm, 4 miles north of Oil City, passing through the sites of several boom towns and some lovely countryside. You can board at the Drake Well Museum, at the Perry Street Station in Titusville, or, on the southern end of the trip, at Rynd Farm, north of Oil City. Operating days are Saturday and Sunday early May to mid-June; Friday, Saturday, and Sunday mid-June through late August; Saturday and Sunday from the end of August through late September; and Friday, Saturday, and Sunday (for autumn foliage) from early October to early November. The schedule of northbound and southbound trains is complicated, may change without notice, and includes additional trains scheduled for special celebration weeks in the summer; moreover, you need advance tickets to guarantee that you'll have a place on the train. To learn what the schedule will be when you plan your visit, write OC & T RR, P.O. Box 68, Oil City 16301, or call (814) 827–2797 or (814) 676–1733. Ticket prices are moderately high.

If you'd like to make part of the same trip on bicycle, try the 10-mile paved trail along Oil Creek from Petroleum Center to Drake Well Park. You can rent bikes at the Egbert Farm Oil Office—Bike Rental (814–677–6907), open daily from 11:00 A.M. to 7:00 P.M., weather permitting. The trail is open from 8:00 A.M. to dark.

If that's still not enough variety, you can arrange a canoe trip lasting from $1\frac{1}{2}$ hours to 5 days daily from mid-April to mid-October from Hallston Marine Canoe Livery. All the streams are class I, no whitewater. For full details and reservations, write Star Route Box 32, Sugarcreek Drive, Franklin 16323 or call (814) 432–3449.

As for interesting places to stay after all this activity, the bed-and-breakfast concept is just beginning to take hold in this area. Kathy and Larry Fasenmyer, in Oil City, have remodeled a 1904 Victorian house to become **Oil Country Inn,** furnished with a mixture of contemporary and antique family furniture, accented with the couple's various collections, including a framed assortment of orange-crate labels. An outstanding feature of the house is a fine stained-glass window in the turret. The moderate price of the room includes a bang-up full breakfast. Kathy, a cookbook fanatic, has been collecting recipes for years. One of her most successful breakfasts is buckwheat pancakes with a topping of yogurt and spiced peaches, and her neighbors would kill for her peach muffin recipe. Ask for instructions to the house when you make reservations (814–677–2638).

Scarely a stone's throw away, on Route 8, 2 miles south of Franklin, the **DeBence Antique Music Museum** provides a more amusing kind of history. The museum has more than 250 antique music boxes, including a rare Berry Wood, Style A.O.W. Automatic, Orchestra—an automatic player that produces the sounds of thirteen different instruments. Jake and Elizabeth DeBence play all the nickelodeons, band organs, orchestrions, and music boxes, and provide guided tours of the museum. They also buy and sell other antiques, including lamps, old toys, trains, and furniture. The museum is open May 1 through October 1, Monday through Saturday, 10:00 A.M. to 5:00 P.M. and Sundays 1:00 P.M. to 5:00 P.M. Call (814) 437–6301 for details; a moderate admission fee is charged.

Lake Country

The drive from Pittsburgh to Erie takes about four hours on Interstate 79, if you don't stop anywhere along the way to explore, but once you get into Erie County, whatever route you've taken, it's almost like being in a different country. As an Erie resident likes to say, "You can't get more off the beaten path than Erie." The sense comes from the facts that Ohio, Lake Erie, and New York form the western, northern, and eastern borders of the county and that getting to Erie from anywhere in Pennsylvania means driving through miles and miles and miles of woodland

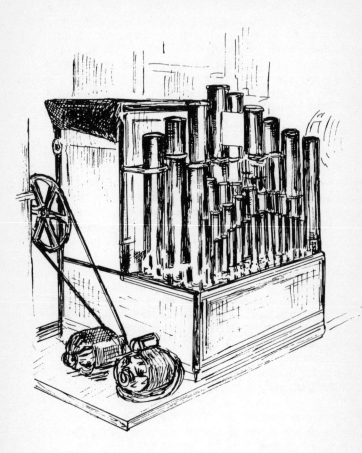

DeBence Antique Music Museum

and uninhabited countryside. But once you get there, you'll find a lot of fun and history in the area.

Less than twenty years ago, suggesting a pleasure trip to Lake Erie would have sounded like a big joke. People had a grim saying: "Dreary Erie, the mistake by the lake." Fish kills kept many of the beaches unpleasant. Snapshots from those years show people standing on the beaches up to their knees in soap suds. Old fishermen who remembered when fish were so plentiful you could catch them with nothing but spaghetti for bait couldn't pull out anything but trash fish. The lake had been pronounced dead. But the problem was actually too much of the wrong kinds of life. Nutrients such as phosphates and nitrates, especially plentiful in agricultural runoff, encouraged excessive growth of algae, which grew so fast that they choked out other forms of plant life and fish life. The process is called *eutrification.* In bad water where no oxygen can reach the bottom, the only fish that can live are the small pan fish. As Lake Erie deteriorated, only pan fish were surviving.

A massive combined effort by area manufacturing companies, local colleges, state and federal government, and concerned citizens turned things around. The city of Erie has improved its sewage disposal system. The Department of Health tests for harmful bacteria regularly. Industries treat their wastes so they won't hurt the lake. Colleges run ecology projects continuously monitoring the state of the water. At least one Erie councilman pilots his boat, at cost, for the monitoring teams.

Game fish began returning to the waters. The city celebrated, with big headlines in the newspaper, when the first coho salmon was caught after the long empty spell. Perhaps part of the success story comes from the central role Lake Erie plays in the lives of the people who live there. Hundreds of people go to the public dock in the city every day, if not to fish, at least to check out conditions. Adults who've lived here all their lives talk about having gone out fishing every morning before school or in the evening after school every day; they do the same today with their own children. This spirit affects what it feels like to visit the lakeshores. The passion is contagious.

The best place to begin learning about Erie and the lake is **Presque Isle State Park.** If you remember your French, you know that *Presque Isle* means "almost an island." One of the most remarkable places in Pennsylvania, it offers enough to keep you busy for weeks. It's a 3,200-acre peninsula extending from the city of Erie into Lake Erie. Interestingly, the combined effects of erosion on one side and sand deposits on the other change the peninsula's shape and location noticeably, not in thousands of years, but in just a few. The **Nature Center** in the park displays maps showing the changes. It's estimated that the peninsula has moved about $1/2$ mile east in the past hundred years. Of course, that doesn't make it any harder to find. Nearly 5 million people visit Presque Isle in a good year. Yet if you avoid the peak summer swimming season, it's possible to walk for hours along the beaches and in the woods without seeing another human being.

For naturalists, part of the attraction is the approximately 300 species of birds and 500 species of ferns and flowering plants. Two undeveloped areas, the **Ecological Reservation** and **Gull Point Sanctuary,** are a naturalist's dream. The best way to get acquainted with the possibilities is to study the displays and literature in the Nature Center, where you'll also find less demanding exhibits, such as those of butterflies and ducks, for children. But children are more likely to want to head for the beaches, where the surf is usually high enough to be interesting without getting so rough in good weather as to be dangerous. At the **East Boat Livery** you can rent rowboats, canoes, and motorboats. The park is open from dawn to dusk. For more details about winter-sports concessions, guided nature tours, movies, and lectures, as well as Nature Center hours, phone (814) 871–4251. To get to the peninsula from Interstate 79, take the 26th Street exit, turn left, and continue to Route 823, which is Peninsula Drive. From Erie, go west on West 12th Street to Peninsula Drive.

In the city of Erie, visit the restored **Flagship Niagara,** one of three American warships surviving from the War of 1812. It commemorates the victory on September 10, 1813, when nine American ships defeated the British fleet on Lake Erie. The ship is at 80 State Street, on Presque Isle Bay and is open Tuesday through Saturday, 9:00 A.M. to 5:00 P.M. and Sunday, noon to 5:00 P.M. Phone (814) 871–4596.

Another action-oriented display is the **Firefighters Historical Museum** at 428 Chestnut Street, which is in the old #4 Erie Firehouse. It contains more than 1,300 items of fire department memorabilia, including old uniforms and equipment and an 1830 hand pumper. The museum is open May through August 10:00 A.M. to 5:00 P.M. on Saturday and 1:00 P.M. to 5:00 P.M. Sunday;

September through October the museum is open from 1:00 P.M. to 5:00 P.M. Saturday and Sunday. Call (814) 456–5969.

Also in the city, **Erie Historical Museum and Planetarium,** housed in a twenty-four-room mansion from the late 1800s, at 356 West 6th Street, has exhibits on regional and maritime history, including the battle of Lake Erie. In other rooms are changing exhibits from the museum collections, decorative arts, and period rooms with outstanding woodwork and stained glass. The planetarium, in the mansion carriage house, recreates the movements of the sun, moon, planets, and stars. The museum is open Tuesday through Sunday, 1:00 P.M. to 5:00 P.M.; the planetarium showings are Saturday at 2:00 P.M., Sunday 2:00 P.M. and 3:00 P.M., and Tuesday through Friday at 2:00 P.M. Additional hours are scheduled for the museum and planetarium in the summer; call (814) 453–5811.

Follow Route 5 east, which parallels the waterfront, through town. This is East Lake Road. Just outside of town, at 5735 East Lake Road, the **Waterfall Restaurant,** built beside a pretty stream, offers inexpensive to moderately priced meals in a comfortable setting. In addition to luncheon specials, including nice salads and a good assortment of seafood and meat entrees, the restaurant sells marvelous local fried perch for lunch and dinner. Ask to sit on the sun porch, from which you can see the waterfall and enjoy the trees. The restaurant is open Monday through Friday from 11:30 A.M. to 1:30 P.M. for lunch and 4:00 P.M. to 9:00 P.M. for dinner; Saturday from 4:00 P.M. to 9:00 P.M. for dinner only; and Sunday from noon to 8:00 P.M. for dinner; phone (814) 899–8173.

In the same neighborhood, **Shades Beach Township Park** at Harbor Creek is a quiet, uncrowded little park with a lake beach and a playground for children that makes a nice place to stop and get some exercise, fish a little, or enjoy the lake. The park is open from 8:00 A.M. to 10:00 P.M.

Wine Country

Continuing east for about 13 more miles brings you to the little rural town of North East, home of four wineries and some interesting historic sites. From Route 5, Route 89 runs down to the **Freeport Public Beach** on Lake Erie. North East is also just a few minutes drive on Route 89 from Interstate 90, if you are not coming from the city of Erie. Driving along the countryside here you'll see acres and acres of vineyards. Lake Erie's wine region stretches about 100 miles along the coast, extending only about 5 miles inland. Wine grapes flourish here because the lake creates a microclimate in which cold spring winds off the lake keep the plants from budding too early and being vulnerable to frost. In the summer, lake breezes cool the vineyards and keep the air circulating, and in the fall, the stored summer warmth from the lake delays frost. Because the lake once was much larger and has receded, the soils along the shore are especially fertile.

Penn Shore Vineyards is just off Route 5, at 10225 East Lake Road, North East. Signs direct you. The winery offers tours and tasting. In addition to their premium vintage wines and a good, dry champagne, Penn Shore Vineyards is known for its specialty wine, Kir, a blend that includes black currant liqueur. The winery and salesroom are open June through October, Monday through Saturday from 9:00 A.M. to 8:00 P.M. and Sunday from noon to 6:00 P.M.; November through May the hours are the same, except closing time is 5:00 P.M. Monday through Saturday. Phone (814) 725–8688.

Mazza Winery, located in a restored eighteenth-century barn overlooking Lake Erie and surrounded by Mazza Vineyards, especially encourages visitors for the Labor Day weekend wine festival, which includes grape stomping, wine tasting, vineyard hay wagon rides, and tours. September, when most grape picking is done, is another interesting time to visit, though the winery offers tours year-round. Mazza Winery offers tours, tasting, and sales, and is open from July through September, Monday through Saturday, 9:00 A.M. to 8:00 P.M.; from October to June the winery closes at 5:30 P.M. It is open Sundays from noon to 4:30 P.M. year-round. Phone (814) 725–8695.

Farther back from the lake, at Interstate 90 (Exit 12) and Route 20, Heritage Wine Cellars is notable because in addition to its list of about thirty white, red, specialty, and carbonated wines, they have Gladwin, a unique, European-style white wine grown from Gladwin grapes on a one-acre plot known as "the boss's acre." The Bostwick family has been nurturing this difficult grape since prohibition, when it had to be called a table grape for its growing to be legal. Heritage Wine Cellars is open Monday through Thursday 9:00 A.M. to 6:00 P.M.; Friday and Saturday, 9:00 A.M. to 8:00 P.M.; and Sunday, 10:00 A.M. to 6:00 P.M. Winter hours may vary slightly. Phone (814) 725–8015.

Also just off Route 20, west of Route 89, at 9440 Buffalo Road, Presque Isle Wine Cellars sells not only finished wines, but also grape juice in season and wine-making supplies (and advice) for the home wine maker. Their outstanding, prize-winning wines are a 1986 Chardonnay and a 1980 Cabernet Sauvignon. The winery is open daily, 8:00 A.M. to 5:00 P.M. except Sunday. Phone (814) 725–1314.

When you're done tasting and touring, consider a meal or even spending the night at **Brown's Village Inn,** Erie County's first country inn, at 51 East Mainstreet in downtown North East. The 1832 Federal-style, red brick building was originally built as a home. It also served as a stagecoach tavern, an underground railroad station, a schoolhouse, and a private nursing home before its current incarnation as a country inn. The restaurant has three dining rooms, one with a library, one overlooking a grape arbor and herb garden, the third looking out on the main street. Meals emphasize fresh local produce in season, good salads, and a special poppy-seed dressing. Luncheon favorites include chicken and biscuits and chef salad; dinner features include veal with brandy and oranges and oriental beef, in addition to steaks and seafood. The three guest rooms are moderately priced and are named for grapes of the region: Niagara, Steuben, and Concord. Rates include full breakfast. At the restaurant, lunch is served Tuesday through Saturday, 11:30 A.M. to 2:00 P.M.; dinner, Tuesday through Thursday, 5:30 P.M. to 8:30 P.M. and Friday and Saturday, 5:30 P.M. to 9:00 P.M. Sunday brunch is served from noon to 3:00 P.M. Phone (814) 725–5522.

While you're in North East, stop at the **Hornby School Museum,** at 10000 Colt Station Road (Route 430) to visit the restored one-room schoolhouse in the style of the 1870s. With a reservation you can arrange to experience the kind of lessons that would have been part of a typical school day. The school is open on Sundays from May through October, 1:00 P.M. to 5:00 P.M. Call (814) 725–5680 for more information.

More fun than school, perhaps, **Lake Shore Railway Museum,** at Wall and Robinson Streets, still has a lot to teach. Two children cried all the way there one morning because they hate museums, but at 5:00 P.M., attendants had to chase the kids out of the train cars to close up. The museum displays historical railroad items from the nineteenth and twentieth centuries, ranging from dining car china to signaling devices. Outside the museum, which is in a station house by the tracks, you may tour a caboose and railroad cars on the siding—a Pullman sleeping car, a diner, freight car, coach, baggage car, and caboose. The wooden caboose is kept as it used to be when it was in service, with a stove and cooking area. In front of the station is an old fireless steamer locomotive, built in Erie in 1937. The museum is open May and September, Saturday and Sunday, 1:00 P.M. to 5:00 P.M. and June through August, Wednesday through Sunday, 1:00 P.M. to 5:00 P.M. Phone (814) 825–2724.

Western Pennsylvania Wineries

Conneaut Cellars Winery
Route 322, R.D. #1
Conneaut Lake, PA 16316
(814) 382–3999

Hillcrest Winery, Ltd.
R.D. #5, Box 301
Greensburg, PA 15601
(412) 832–5720

Francesco Winery
R.D. #1 Box 1781
Russell, PA 16345
Phone not listed

Lapic Winery
682 Tulip Drive
New Brighton, PA 15066
(412) 846–2031

Heritage Wine Cellars
12101 East Main Road
North East, PA 16412
(814) 725–8105

Mazza Vineyards
11815 Lake Road
North East, PA 16424
(814) 725–8695

Heritage Wine Cellars
North Vandergrift
R.D. #1 Route 66,
Apollo and Vandergrift
North Vandergrift, PA 15690
(412) 568–3518

Penn-Shore Vineyards, Inc.
10225 East Lake Road
North East, PA 16824
(814) 725–8688

Presque Isle Wine Cellars
9440 Buffalo Road
North East, PA 16428
(814) 725–1314

Heritage Wine Cellars
Latrobe
Box 333, Route 30
Latrobe, PA 15650
(412) 539–3711

Sara Coyne Wine Cellars
7650 Bargain Road

Erie, PA 16509
(814) 833–4560

Shuster Cellars, Inc.
2900 Turkey Farm Road
Irwin, PA 15642
(412) 351–0979
(412) 864–4691

Sweet Williams Mountain Winery
39 Mefferks Run Road
Wilcox, PA 15870
Phone not listed

Whispering Valley
Wine Cellars
R.D. #1 Box 1267
Old Pittsburgh Road
Wampum, PA 16157
Phone not listed

Windgate Vineyards
R.D. #2 Box 213
Smicksburg PA 16525
(814) 257–8797

Benfer's Museum

Off the Beaten Path in Central Pennsylvania

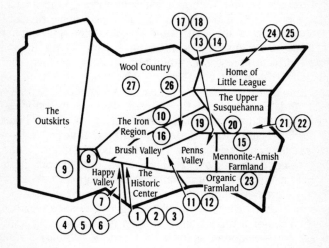

1. Duffy's Tavern
2. Pennsylvania Military Museum
3. Boal Mansion and Museum and the Christopher Columbus Family Chapel
4. Tavern Restaurant
5. The Nittany Lion Inn
6. The Corner Room
7. The Earth and Mineral Sciences Museum
8. Central Pennsylvania Village Crafts
9. Eutaw House
10. Curtin Village
11. Millheim Hotel
12. Woodward Cave
13. Woodward Inn
14. Benfer's Museum
15. Mifflinburg Buggy Museum
16. Penn's Cave
17. Fisher's Harness Shop
18. Madisonburg Bake Shop
19. Brush Valley Greenhouse
20. Bechtel's Pennsylvania Cheesemaker Retail Store
21. Lewisburg Hotel
22. Packwood House Museum
23. Walnut Acres
24. Peter J. McGovern Little League Baseball Museum
25. Reighard House Bed and Breakfast Inn
26. Woolrich Store
27. Cohick's Trading Post

Central Pennsylvania

The long-standing joke about central Pennsylvania, especially Centre County, has been that it is equally inaccessible from all points. You must drive several miles in any direction before you come to a major city.

One of the most pleasant sections to visit for a combination of scenery, good food, and historic interest is the village of Boalsburg, home of the first Memorial Day ceremonies, 3 miles east of State College on Business Route 322. The town was originally a stagecoach stop at the foot of Tussey Mountain, but until the early 1960s, when many area residents became increasingly interested in historic restoration and preservation, the town didn't seem to be much but deteriorating, albeit historic, old houses, cheap rentals for students from nearby Pennsylvania State University. Today virtually all the houses have been restored to picture-book prettiness; specialty shops occupy the fine old buildings on the historic diamond; and **Duffy's Tavern,** once an 1819 stagecoach tavern, now furnished with antiques, serves steaks, seafood, drinks, and at lunch, a good bean soup. Its atmosphere is unique in that it manages to be both a local bar and a place for gracious dining. It's worth noting that Duffy's history was part of the tavern's ambience long before such emphasis became a national rage. Duffy's is open for lunch 11:30 A.M. to 2:00 P.M. and for dinner, 5:00 P.M. to 10:00 P.M. Monday through Saturday. Hours on Sunday are 1:00 P.M. to 9:00 P.M. Phone (814) 466-6241.

Among the shops on the diamond, The Country Sampler, featuring fine cookware and serving pieces as well as all kinds of needlework supplies, is one of the best established and most tasteful. It is open daily 9:30 A.M. to 5:00 P.M. and Thursday to 8:00 P.M. Phone (814) 466-7402.

Across the street, Gifts by Tom Horner, started by a master decorator in the area more than a decade ago, fills a beautifully restored seven-room house built in 1811. The merchandise includes country table linens, baskets, and tinware and there are a Christmas room and a children's room. Hours are Monday through Saturday, 10:00 A.M. to 5:00 P.M.

When shopping palls, cross Route 322 to visit the **Pennsylvania Military Museum,** where exhibits and collections illustrate Pennsylvania's participation in wars from the French and Indian

War through World War II. The displays include collections of artifacts from the French and Indian War, dioramas depicting battles of the War for Independence and the War of 1812, and uniforms and equipment from the Mexican and Civil Wars. But by far the most spectacular exhibit is the life-sized reproduction of part of a World War I battlefield in France, complete with uniformed "soldiers," trenches, cannon, tank, and truck, through which visitors walk, eerily surrounded by simulated artillery flashes and battle sounds. The museum is open weekdays except Monday from 10:00 A.M. to 5:00 P.M. and Sunday, 1:00 P.M. to 5:00 P.M. From October through April closing time is 4:30 P.M. Closed on some holidays. Phone (814) 466–6263.

Outside the museum, the 28th Division Shrine, begun by Colonel Theodore Boal and fellow members of the 28th Division Officer's Club, memorializes the men of Pennsylvania's 28th Division in World War I. A broad expanse of lawn and some picnic facilities make this a pleasant area to rest or let children run.

Directly across Route 322, on old 322, the **Boal Mansion and Museum and the Christopher Columbus Family Chapel** offer fascinating glimpses of the acquisitions and lives of the Boal family. The mansion was built partly by David Boal in 1789 and finished by his son, David, for whom Boalsburg is named, and finally enlarged by Colonel Theodore Davis Boal in 1898. In these consecutive changes it grew from an early stone cabin to its present grandeur. Inside are fine woodwork and mantels, early American and European furniture, art, china, glass and silver— the accumulation of nine generations of Boal family furnishings. The chapel belonged to the Columbus family in Spain. The Boal family imported it to Pennsylvania in 1919. In addition to sixteenth- and seventeenth-century woodwork and artwork, the chapel displays church equipment—ancient vestments, chalices, large candlesticks, and statues. The most unusual part of the display is two larges pieces of the True Cross with an Episcopal letter certifying its history. Other buildings on the property contain varied American, French, and Spanish military and domestic relics, some dating from medieval times. The site is open every day except Tuesdays from 2:00 P.M. to 5:00 P.M. from May 1 to June 1 and Labor Day through October 31 and from 10:00 A.M. to 5:00 P.M. June 8 through Labor Day. The admission fee is moderate. No children under 6. For more details write Curator, Columbus Chapel—Boal Museum, Boalsburg 16827 or call (814) 466–6210.

In a more contemporary mode, if you're in the area on a Tuesday from mid-June through October, you can browse through the Boalsburg Farmers Market's produce, plants, and baked goods, then return to Route 322 to eat at The Boalsburg Steak House, which, though not historic, is a long-time tradition and favored eating place among locals. You can't miss it because of the larger-than-life bull on the roof. When the bull first went up, a dozen or so years ago, it immediately became a local joke, and stealing it has been an occasional prank. It's now so much a part of the landscape that the Boalsburg Steak House uses it as a part of their advertising logo. The steak house serves more than twenty different cuts and sizes of steak, along with seafood and a salad bar. The steak house (814–466–6251) has complete bar service and is open Monday through Saturday 4:30 P.M. to 9:30 P.M. and Sunday 3:00 P.M. to 8:30 P.M.

Happy Valley

The main campus of the Pennsylvania State University is at State College, a town that takes its name from days in 1874 when the Agricultural College of Pennsylvania became the Pennsylvania State College. The area calls itself "Happy Valley." It tells you something about the place to know that although much confusion comes from the fact that Pennsylvania State University's address is University Park, and few outsiders understand that State College is the name of the town *around* the university, residents have steadfastly refused to change the name of the town. It has too much traffic and too many people to be considered a secluded getaway, but because of the influence of the university and the kinds of people who are attracted to such places, spending time here can be fun, especially if you avoid football season. The town and university are isolated in rural countryside. Moreover, the location is central to many other interesting spots. To experience the long-standing traditions of the town, you need to dine at the Tavern Restaurant, hoist a beer at the All American Rathskeller, or the Post House Tavern, spend the night at the Nittany Lion Inn, and breakfast at The Corner Room, preferably in a window seat.

The **Tavern Restaurant** was opened by a Penn State graduate who didn't want to leave town. For years it was the only "nice" place to go for a special dinner. It was a favorite with students, who ordered the famous Tavern spaghetti for a dollar, and with faculty, who could afford the steaks and chicken. Even though State College now has many good restaurants, the Tavern remains a nostalgic favorite with local residents and visiting alumni. It's the one restaurant that still feels tweedy and slightly academic. Many of the waiters and waitresses are students; many of the patrons are faculty and long-time residents. The spaghetti is now five or six times that early price, but dinners are still moderately priced. Originally only beer could be served in State College but the Tavern now has complete bar service. It is open for dinner 5:00 P.M. to 11:00 P.M. daily and until midnight Friday and Saturday. You'll find it on southbound State Route 26, 220 East College Avenue; call (814) 238–6116 for more information.

The All-American Rathskeller, 108 South Pugh Street, is just "the Skeller" to people who go there. Only a couple of blocks from the wall of campus, it's been a college watering hole since 1933. Generations of students, local ex-students, faculty, and friends of all these have met around the huge booth tables regularly, giving themselves names such as "The Friday Frolic Club," and ordering "a couple a rocks," meaning two pony-sized bottles of Rolling Rock Beer, always at a special price. People who check such things claim that the same graffiti has been on the bathroom walls since 1933. Call (814) 237–3858 for information.

Although students do go to the Post House Tavern, located next to the railroad tracks at 46 North Atherton Street, it is more a gathering place for older working people. As for food, the Post House specializes in live lobster and, in season, fresh oysters, as well as other seafood. The atmosphere is just plain bar, but it's friendly and it's got character.

Conversely, **The Nittany Lion Inn** (814–237–7671) just across North Atherton, is the epitome of university gentility. The inn is a good-sized, slightly worn hotel with dining rooms and meeting rooms on the Penn State campus, operated by the university's hotel administration college. It's a favorite place to bunk visiting speakers, seminar participants, and the like. It's quiet, the beds are good, and the atmosphere utterly unfrenetic, toned down by leather chairs, comfortable furniture, and noncommercial-looking carpets.

The Corner Room, in the old State College Hotel, at the corner of Allen Street and College Avenue, where the campus mall meets College Avenue, is a sort of hub and meeting point for town and campus people. It's *the* spot for breakfast, especially for a Corner Room sticky bun. Because the building is on the corner, seating along two long walls looks directly onto the sidewalks, where breakfasters and passersby openly watch each other. If you're there around 10:00 A.M. most days, you'll probably see a handsome, white bearded gentleman who looks a lot like Arthur Treacher sitting at a small inside booth, writing. Gil Aberg has been writing (and greeting friends) in the Corner Room for so long he's become part of the tradition. If you speak to him, he'll certainly respond and charm you with his erudition.

It's easy to leave from here to go sightseeing on the Penn State campus, which begins just across the street. Among the possibilities, two are special. **The Earth and Mineral Sciences Museum** in the Steidle Building on Pollock Road exhibits minerals, fossils, and gemstones, as well as paintings showing the development of the mineral industries in Pennsylvania. The exhibit highlight is a display of fluorescent minerals where the viewer pushes buttons to light them and show how they react. The museum is open Tuesday through Friday, 9:00 A.M. to 5:00 P.M. and Saturday and Sunday, 1:00 P.M. to 5:00 P.M. It is closed Monday. Farther back on the campus, Ag Hill has entertained countless children with its animal barns, deer pens, and creamery ice cream cones. For adults, the flower gardens are a delight in blooming season. Also, as you walk up the mall from College Avenue onto the center of campus, you'll pass the Penn State obelisk—a tall spire built of stone samples from all over Pennsylvania. According to campus legend, it will fall when a virgin walks by.

Back in the town proper, among the myriad changing and student-oriented shops, at 206 South Allen Street, The Silver Cellar, a second-floor sales gallery featuring the work of local goldsmiths in silver, gold, and other metals, offers an appealing collection of contemporary, handcrafted jewelry. They are open regular business hours, Monday though Saturday; Call (814) 237-1566 for more information.

Just outside the downtown area, on Route 26, 1011 East College Avenue, **Central Pennsylvania Village Crafts,** a crafts cooperative that began in 1971, offers some remarkable handwork at moderate prices. The organization represents a lovely success story, to which you contribute when you purchase any of the crafts. The purpose of the organization is to help rural people in central Pennsylvania earn extra money through their craft work by providing them training, supplies, and a market. Membership numbers over 150 craftspeople, mainly rural women who work at home and live on fixed incomes. The program includes training programs in traditional crafts for beginners and workshops in advanced techniques for experienced people. In addition to providing supplementary income, the program aims to preserve the northern Appalachian crafts heritage. The sales gallery on East College Avenue is an important outlet for all these efforts, but the cooperative members ship to specialty shops all over the country, including some fine museum gift shops. This is a nice opportunity to buy the kind of handwork you admire but don't have time to create yourself, with the added pleasure of knowing that you're helping the craftspeople and securing a cultural tradition at the same time. The merchandise ranges from wooden items and crocheted snowflake Christmas tree ornaments (some of which have hung on the White House Christmas tree) to elaborate, full-sized quilts. The shop is open 10:00 A.M. to 5:30 P.M. Monday through Friday and 10:00 A.M. to 2:00 P.M. Saturday. Phone (814) 234–0933 for further information.

The Outskirts

While you're in the State College–Boalsburg area, you might want to plan dinner one evening at the **Eutaw House,** a long-established restaurant in an old colonial inn built in 1823. It's the kind of place to go to for a special occasion. Part of its charm is that if you make a reservation in advance you can arrange private dining even for as few as two. The menu features aged beef and gourmet seafood. Cocktails and wine are available. The Eutaw House (814–364–1039) is in Potters Mills, 13 miles east of State College, at the intersection of Routes 322 and 144. There's nothing else around, so going there really is a separate excursion. Hours are 11:00 A.M. to 11:00 P.M. daily.

An outdoor area worth investigating on the other side of State College is The Barrens and Scotia Pond, 4 miles west on Route 322. The Shawnee Indians gave it the name because nothing much grows in the sandy acid clay except scrub oak and blueberries. The site is interesting because the life that does persist here includes a number of rare and endangered species, such as the rare buck moth, as well as deer, grouse, and wild turkeys. Indeed, unless you have a bulletproof suit it's better to avoid the Barrens during hunting season. Now protected State Game Land, this is the last barren left in Pennsylvania. Much of the adjacent area also was known as barrens less than half a century ago, when teenagers favored it as a place to go and watch the "submarine races" at night. That adjacent area now is a fully established housing development about thirty years old, in which the scrub oak defied naturalists' gloomy predictions of death and instead grew tall enough to make the place overly shady. Scotia Pond and the clay pits in the Barrens attract visitors because of an abundance of wildlife and wild flowers, as well as some historic interest, since it is the site of an iron-ore mine built by Andrew Carnegie in the 1800s. The most interesting single feature of the area, however, is probably its freakishly cold temperatures. The ground here absorbs cold, so that in winter, temperatures may drop to as low as thirty or forty degrees below zero, regardless of the weather in the surrounding area. Even in summer, temperatures can be as much as thirty degrees lower than those elsewhere in the region. To get there, turn onto Scotia Road from Route 322 and go slightly less than a mile.

The Iron Region

Milesburg, a community of about 1,500 people, just off Interstate 80 where it is joined by Route 220, isn't particularly close to anything, but it's worth a little time to drive there from State College or to stop off when you're crossing the state on Interstate 80 to visit **Curtin Village.** This is an old iron village that has gradually been restored so that you can visit the buildings that were part of the original complex.

In this part of the country, ironmasters ruled their villages like monarchies, and, while some must have been benevolent, the old books are full of stories of their tempers and cruelty. One of the worst stories is of an ironmaster becoming angry with his dogs and in a rage driving them into the burning furnace. At this particular site, the ironmaster was Roland Curtin. His family home, Curtin mansion, a fourteen-room random fieldstone house in the late Empire style, has been restored and furnished as closely as possible to the way it was when he lived in it in the mid-1800s.

On the circular staircase inside you can see where generations of Curtins have worn the treads concave. Curtin is still a well-known family name in the area, so much information and history has been available. Also restored are the blacksmith shop, forge, furnace, company store, and railway station. There are a number of log homes in which ironworkers used to live. One was still occupied by an elderly worker until just a few years ago.

A unique feature of the village is that it remained in the Curtin family from 1810 to 1921, when Eagle Furnace "blew out." This was the last cold-blast charcoal iron furnace to operate in the United States. Restoration of the home began when the H. L. Curtin family presented the home to the Roland Curtin Foundation for one dollar.

Guided tours include information about Centre County ironmasters and the role of the iron industry in area development, as well as much information about the Curtin family and how the village operated. It is open Tuesday through Saturday, 10:00 A.M. to 4:00 P.M. and Sunday, 1:00 P.M. to 5:00 P.M. from Memorial Day to October. During October, hours are 1:00 P.M. to 5:00 P.M. Saturday and Sunday. Admission is $3 for adults and $1 for children. Call (814) 355–1982. Curtin is 3 miles northeast of Interstate 80 from exit 23, on State Route 150.

Penns Valley

From Boalsburg, Route 45 meets Route 322, taking you east to Centre Hall and Old Fort and two of the most scenic, picturesque, and interesting drives in Pennsylvania. One is from Centre Hall to Lewisburg on Route 192; the other is from Old Fort, just outside Centre Hall, to Lewisburg on Route 45. Because the two roads parallel each other, to enjoy them both you must backtrack or make a loop. Either way, it's worth the time. Information here is given to proceed from Centre Hall and Old Fort to Lewisburg; you can easily reverse the directions for either trip. Route 45 is the more heavily traveled road and carries some truck traffic, but it's a good road and easy driving. Route 192 is less traveled, more winding, slower, and takes you through a number of charming villages and an area of Amish farms and small shops, in addition to Raymond B. Winter State Park.

Driving from Old Fort east about half an hour on Route 45,

you'll find Millheim, a lively farming town with some lovely old houses along or near the main street, which is Route 45. **The Millheim Hotel,** a 200-year-old inn on the main street, is interesting to look at and fun to visit. Its character is somewhat schizophrenic because some local farmers and businessmen gather at the bar here after work, but it also attracts dressed-up diners from State College and Lewisburg. The dining room serves full dinners Friday, Saturday, and Sunday, including some unusual recipes from the Moosewood Cookbook and two vegetarian entrees, as well as steaks, seafood, a superior salad bar, and a dessert bar. On Friday and Saturday dinner is served from 5:00 P.M. to 9:30 P.M. and on Sunday, from 1:00 P.M. to 8:00 P.M. The dining room is open seven days a week to serve sandwiches (with homemade bread if you want it) and platters. If you'd like an inexpensive place to spend the night, the hotel has seventeen nicely renovated guest rooms, carpeted and furnished with antiques, on the second and third floors. The rooms share baths and do not have television or telephones. The hotel serves a full country breakfast in the morning. Phone (814) 349–5994.

No more than a mile down the road, you'll pass through the little village of Aaronsburg, about which a book once was written because it was founded as a community where people of differing religions intended to coexist in harmony. Nobody could have foreseen that the tolerance would eventually be called upon to extend also to the Amish, who have migrated into the area. It's worth driving slowly through this little town because it is so perfectly kept, with its old homes in such fine repair, you feel as though you're moving through a scene from a postcard.

Approximately 5 miles farther, you'll come to Woodward, where **Woodward Cave,** one of the largest stalagmite caves in the state, offers hour-long guided walking tours through the five rooms of the cavern. Unlike most such attractions, this one accommodates wheelchairs. To give you an idea of the size of this cave, when a concert was held in the fourth room one Christmas, it was attended by more than 400 people, and there was room for them all to be seated. Take a sweater in the summer. The temperature is always forty-eight degrees. It is open 9:00 A.M. to 7:00 P.M. from mid-May to Labor Day and 9:00 A.M. to 5:00 P.M. the rest of the year. Rates are $6 for adults and $3 for children. Phone (814) 349–9800.

If you like the placidity of the Woodward area well enough to want to hang around, you could stay at the **Woodward Inn,** an 1814 Georgian stone bed and breakfast with eight guest rooms available weekends. It is furnished with four generations of family antiques from Germany and Pennsylvania. Breakfast usually includes something like Pennsylvania Dutch shoofly pie or a crumb cake. The rooms do not have telephones or televisions, and some of the rooms share baths. Phone (814) 349–8118.

Unless you decide to walk through the Hairy John State Forest picnic area nearby and read the story of how it got its name, your next stop might be at Millmont, a mile south of Hartleton off Route 45, to see Marlin and Phyllis **Benfer's Museum.** Their collection of farm machinery, tractors, cars, tools, guns, coins, furniture, glassware, and dishes, numbers over 10,000 pieces and fills five buildings. It takes about three hours to tour everything. Hours are 1:00 P.M. to 8:00 P.M. Sundays from the first of April to November 1; it is open only by appointment in the winter. Admission costs $3.00; phone (717) 922–1810 for further information.

Mennonite-Amish Farmland

Your next stop will also be a step back in time at Mifflinburg. It dates from the end of the American Revolution. The old homes have been restored, painted with an eye to historic authenticity, and buffed to a Victorian perfection that probably exceeds their original state. In the 1800s, Mifflinburg became the "buggy capital" of the country, producing more buggies per capita than any other place in the country. At one time as many as twenty different buggy and sleigh factories were going full tilt in the village. One of them, the Heiss Carriage Works, at 523 Green Street, survives today as the **Mifflinburg Buggy Museum.**

The story of this museum's success is a great testimony to the community spirit of the Mifflinburg townspeople. At the time of the American Bicentennial, they wanted to do something commemorating their town's history. The Heiss buggy works had been abandoned forty years earlier and locked up. The people decided to buy the house, shop, and repository from the family, restore them as a museum, and offer guided tours, all with community volunteers. When they opened up the main shop, they found it looking as though workers had walked off expecting to return the next day. All the equipment and tools were lying where

41

they had last been used. A lunch pail and half a box of shredded wheat still sat on a workbench. Volunteers have restored the home, with most of its original, modest furnishings intact, and put the shop and repository back into operating condition. Demonstrations of the entire buggy-making process and a chance to go through the house are part of the tour. Many of the same people who worked on the restoration guide the tours; no one here is ever bored and slick, reciting from memorized spiels. An added fillip is that some of the people taking the tour with you may be Mennonites or Amish from the area, people for whom buggies are still an important part of life. The museum is open Saturday and Sunday 1:00 P.M. to 5:00 P.M. (the last tour begins at 4:40 P.M.) May through mid-September. Two special events are annual Buggy Days on Saturday and Sunday of Memorial Day weekend and Christmas at the Heiss House the first Sunday of December. Admission is $2.00. Phone (717) 966–0233.

If being in Amish country whets your taste for their handcrafts, stop at Mary Koons at 408 Chestnut Street in Mifflinburg to look at the Amish quilts, dolls, pillows, and other needlework for sale. It is open Monday through Saturday 9:00 A.M. to 5:30 P.M. and until 8:00 P.M. Fridays. Phone (717) 966–0341.

To make the trip to Lewisburg on Route 192, start from Centre Hall. Try to be there either for lunch or dinner at the Mt. Nittany Inn, between Centre Hall and Pleasant Gap on Route 144, at the top of Centre Hall Mountain. For years the Mt. Nittany Inn advertised, "Steak and brew and a breathtaking view." The view's still magnificent; the menu's expanded. In addition to the huge choice of steaks for which the place became known, they offer specialties for dinner, such as lobster pot pie, chicken Marsala, and braised pork tenderloin with a schnapps demi-glaze. At lunch steaks and sandwiches are available. The restaurant is open Monday through Thursday 11:30 A.M. to 9:00 P.M., Friday and Saturday until 10:00 P.M., and on Sunday, brunch is served from 10:00 A.M. to 3:00 P.M. and dinner is served from 5:00 P.M. to 8:00 P.M. The faster menu is available in the Bistro all hours.

Brush Valley

A couple of miles back down the mountain to Centre Hall, begin your trip east on Route 192, with a stop at **Penn's Cave.**

This is too popular an attraction to be considered undiscovered, but it's a unique cave worth being in the company of tourists to see. You tour this limestone, all-water cavern by boat. Geologically, the cave was the bed of a shallow sea millions of years ago. Today the interior of the cavern is carved by the water into colorful stalagmites and stalactites that resemble familiar forms— dragons and the Statue of Liberty, for instance. In legend, the Seneca Indian princess, Nitanee, and her French lover were thrown into the cave to die for defying Indian custom. Historically, it is known that Indians and explorers took shelter in the dry rooms of the cave. Other attractions at Penn's Cave are short airplane rides to see the farmland from the air, a wildlife sanctuary, and a shop featuring antiques and items made in Pennsylvania. In a natural den near the cavern, Boomer, a North American mountain lion, roars at visitors. Penn's Cave is open February 15 to May 31 and September, October, and November, daily from 9:00 A.M. to 5:00 P.M. and June, July, and August, daily 9:00 A.M. to 7:00 P.M. In December, it is open weekends only, 11:00 A.M. to 5:00 P.M. Rates are moderately high. Airplane rides cost $10. Special rates are available for combined cave and flight tickets. Phone (814) 364-1664.

From here, the drive on Route 192 is through rural valleys. More accidents are caused by deer than by other drivers. Be careful. It will probably take you about fifteen minutes to get from Centre Hall to Madisonburg. Following the sign, turn off Route 192 onto the little road that takes you back into the village. On your left, **Fisher's Harness Shop,** owned and operated by Amish and lit with gas lanterns, sells and repairs harnesses for area Amish and also sells a variety of tack for regional horsemen and horsewomen. For customers not involved with large animals, the shop has decorative sheepskins, boots, shoes, and assorted other leather goods. It is open Monday through Saturday, 8:00 A.M. to 5:00 P.M.

An Amish population has collected among the natives all the way from Madisonburg to Mifflinburg. This is farmland. The Amish businesses are all little shops like the harness shop. In addition, many of the women sell produce and eggs from their farmhouses. Simple signs out front will tell you. There are no "see the Amish" commercial attractions of any kind here, nor is it appropriate to stare, ask impudent questions, or try to photograph the Amish people. They don't mind your photographing their farms, barns, and buggies. The people welcome you as a serious customer just as they welcome the local non-Amish population who do business with them. You'll find their English good and their monetary skills excellent.

To clear up another common misconception, although the Amish grow much of what they eat, they generally are not natural-food fans. They drink Kool-Aid, eat Cheerios, make Jell-o, and bake white breads and very sweet pies and cakes. You'll see all this firsthand if you stop in the **Madisonburg Bake Shop** diagonally across the road from the harness shop. The goodies include fresh-baked cakes, pies, including the mandatory shoofly, sticky buns, moon pies, and bread, as well as cider in season, an assortment of handcrafts, and sometimes eggs or produce. The shop is open Monday and Friday 7:00 A.M. to 8:00 P.M. and Thursday and Saturday 7:30 A.M. to 5:00 P.M. and is closed Tuesday, Wednesday, and Sunday.

The bake shop is at the corner of the road. Round the bend and continue following the road to the **Brush Valley Greenhouse,** where you can find vegetable plants, bedding plants, houseplants, and seasonal gift plants. You're welcome to browse as long as you please; hours are 8:00 A.M. to 5:00 P.M.

The road that runs in front of the greenhouse continues around another curve or two, then brings you back out onto Route 192. As you continue toward Rebersburg, you'll pass several more greenhouse signs that point up long dirt lanes to farmsteads against the mountains or along the creek. The names on these change from time to time, but in this part of the state it's a fair bet that anywhere a small commercial greenhouse is established it will continue operating under *somebody's* management. Each of these places is unique. If you're in the mood for exploring paths off *off* the beaten path, drive back a couple of the lanes where you see signs. Drive slowly—the lanes will probably be rough.

In Rebersburg, take a few minutes to stop and look at the old homes and churches along the main (and only complete) street. The state's historical society has been actively photographing them to have a permanent record. As local residents become increasingly interested in historic restoration, they're stripping away sidings and interior changes that were added to "modernize" the old buildings. Be sure to stop in one of the two general stores in town. They're directly opposite one another: Paul's Store and Hettinger's. According to local lore, you patronize the store on the same side of the road as your house. As a traveler, you're at leave to try either one. Hettinger's has a wide candy assortment; Paul carries a little bit of just about everything in the world. Once when a customer asked for goat steaks, he asked, "Do you mean the kind you eat or the kind you drive into the ground?" apparently ready to provide either. If Amish horses are tied in front of the stores, park a few spaces away.

Driving from Rebersburg to Lewisburg takes forty to fifty minutes, longer if you slow down to enjoy the scenery or if you get stuck behind a tractor or buggy for a few miles. The road passes through Raymond B. Winter State Park, one of the prettiest parks, with picturesque streams, rhododendron, and especially nice picnic and swimming facilities, all conveniently near the road.

The Upper Susquehanna

Lewisburg is a town oozing history, on the Susquehanna River. It is the home of Bucknell University, a historic school. As with most towns, however, the history of the town is in the downtown area, not even hinted at by the entrance, a strip city like those on the outskirts of most old business districts. But even on the strip, you'll find more that is appealing to an off-the-beaten-path traveler than in most such commercial areas. Right where Route 192 joins Route 15, and just about half a block north of where Route 45 joins Route 192, a pleasant, inexpensive place to pick up a good meal is Bechtel's Dairy and Restaurant, famous for homemade ice cream, but also serving good sandwiches, homemade soups, homemade pies, and salads, as well as heavier dinner entrees. The Bechtel family started the restaurant in 1923. Today a granddaughter manages the restaurant. The friendly, family feeling persists even though the place is large enough to handle lots of customers at once. You'll recognize the place by the large model cow in front; it's open Monday through Saturday 7:00 A.M. to 10:00 P.M. and Sunday 11:30 A.M. to 10:00 P.M.

In an attached building, **Bechtel's Pennsylvania Cheese-maker Retail Store** sells many different kinds of cheese, including some low-sodium and low-fat varieties, made by Eldore Hanni on the premises. Hanni learned cheesemaking in Wisconsin as a boy, helping his father in his cheese factory. In the ensuing twenty plus years he has learned to make more than forty kinds of specialty natural cheese. He came to Pennsylvania in 1979. Some of his more popular cheeses include Sweetheart Cheese, a mild, soft, white ethnic Greek cheese, and baby Swiss. He also makes cheese curds—a mild longhornlike cheese in soft curds about the size of quarters rather than formed into blocks. For serious lovers of cheese, the curds are about as hard to stop eating as those potato chips in the television commercial. "Bet you can't eat just one!" Lots of samples are always out for tasting. The store will ship orders and accept mail orders and is open Monday through Saturday from 10:00 A.M. to 6:00 P.M. and Sunday from 1:00 P.M. to 6:00 P.M. In January and February hours are shortened to Monday through Thursday and Saturday from 11:00 A.M. to 6:00 P.M., Friday from 11:00 A.M. to 8:00 P.M., and Sunday from 1:00 P.M. to 5:00 P.M. Phone (717) 524–2923.

Of possible places to spend the night in Lewisburg, two are especially pleasant. The University Motor Inn is an older motel between Route 45 and Route 192 on Route 15 where the atmosphere is almost familylike. People working in the area on temporary projects and people waiting to move into permanent homes stay there, as do many regular travelers. Players on softball teams that have games nearby also stay there, but they are not rowdy. Though the rooms are not fancy, they're comfortable, and pets are allowed. The staff is as friendly as the guests. The dining room has a nice breakfast buffet on weekends and serves good, inexpensive Italian entrees at dinner. It is open 7:00 A.M. to 11:00 P.M. The motel's phone number is (717) 523–1171.

For more historic accommodations, try **The Lewisburg Hotel,** a refurbished 150-year-old hotel that has welcomed state governors and the poet Walt Whitman. Fifteen rooms are on the second and third floors of the hotel and eighteen more in the motel addition; The Governors' Room and The Cameron Lounge, in the hotel, offer imaginative continental meals. In the more formal Governors' Room, where the decor centers on late nineteenth-century chestnut and oak paneling and elaborate high ceilings, the extensive menu includes seafoods, steaks, and chicken, prepared with unusual and delicate sauces and seasonings. The Cameron Lounge is friendly, low-key, and casual enough to allow wearing shorts or jeans. The menu is similar to that of the Governors' Room, without some of the more elaborate dishes. The fettuccini, pâté, and salads are outstanding. Wine and cocktails are available. The Governors' Room is open Tuesday through Saturday 5:30 P.M. to 10:00 P.M.; the Cameron Lounge is open Monday through Saturday 5:00 P.M. to 10:00 P.M. Call (717) 523–1216. (Route 45 east, crossing Route 15, becomes Main Street. The hotel is at the intersection of Market and Second streets.)

After a meal or a drink at the Lewisburg Hotel, it's nice to leave your car where it's parked and walk up and down some of the streets to study the restored old homes. A map of historic sites for self-guided tours is available from the Union County Tourist Agency, at 418 Market Street (717–524–2815).

One home you can count on getting to see inside is the **Packwood House Museum,** at 15 North Water Street, right beside the river. It was built in the late 1700s as a tavern and hotel serving travelers along the Susquehanna. They kept enlarging the place until by 1869 it had twenty-six hotel rooms, baggage room, reading room, barroom, dining room, kitchen, sitting room, and parlor. According to local history, the hotel went out of business in 1887, partly because of the temperance movement. Another owner added on to it, converting it all into townhouses.

And then John and Edith Fetherston, Lewisburg natives, bought it. At this point the story ceases to be an average local house history because the Fetherstons were, well, unusual. She considered herself a painter and a collector. He was an engineer who thought that everything she did was just wonderful. Moreover, he made enough money for her to be able to do as she wished. They renamed the property Packwood House after their estate in England and began filling it with the pieces Mrs. Fetherston collected and the pictures she painted. John died in 1962; Edith followed ten years later, leaving the house and everything in trust to be operated as a public museum.

"The result," as one tour guide put it, "is twenty-seven rooms full of stuff." In the Tavern alone, there are 700 items. Mrs. Fetherston apparently collected impulsively and eclectically, buying whatever caught her eye when she traveled. The result is a mixture of fine pieces and near junk that make touring the house much more fun than visiting museums where you spend all your time in awe. Real people with real personalities come alive at this place. Here a huge Tiffany chandelier is in the same room with a copper brazier that was probably used for cooking in the desert, with a conch shell to blow into to summon servants, with a dentist's chair to—who knows what? Items range from quality reproductions and good antiques to handcrafted regional items. You'll find more glass, china, silver, and crystal in the cupboards than in most gift shops.

Strangely, although Mrs. Fetherston did not have children and is said not to have cared for them, she collected children's furniture, dolls, books, doll furniture, and toys. It's all here. Her paintings are all here, too. One of the reasons John wanted the house to become a museum after he died was so that there would be a place to display her paintings. Among them are surrealistic, pastel flower arrangements, sometimes seeming to float on the canvas because she didn't paint in the horizon line. She painted a series of pictures featuring her white chickens. One, of a rooster in the yard with two hens, is entitled, "The Bridegroom Cometh."

In establishing the museum, the trustees put in a glass case behind which you can see exposed parts of the original structure. You can pick up some quality handcrafted items in the museum gift shop. Museum hours are Tuesday through Friday, 10:00 A.M. to 5:00 P.M.; Saturday, 1:00 P.M. to 5:00 P.M.; Sunday, 2:00 P.M. to 5:00 P.M. The last tour begins at 4:00 P.M., and it is closed Mondays and holidays. The admission fee is moderate. Call (717) 524-0323 for information.

Another place to pick up unusual gifts is Colonial Candlecrafters, a workshop and salesroom where you'll find all kinds of handmade candles, including some that are hand painted and many that are designed for specific special occasions, such as weddings. You can also buy supplies to make your own candles here. On some days you may tour the workshop. Colonial Candlecrafters is on U.S. Route 15, 6½ miles south of Interstate 80 Exit 30 South and is open Monday through Thursday, Saturday, and Sunday from 10:00 A.M. to 5:30 P.M. and Friday to 9:00 P.M. The phone number is (717) 524-4556.

Organic Farmland

While you're in the Lewisburg-Mifflinburg area, it's worth taking a side trip to visit **Walnut Acres** in Penns Creek. For more than forty years the Keene family has raised and sold grains, beef, and chickens without pesticides or chemical fertilizers on the Walnut Acres farm. Even if you're not particularly interested in such food, the farm is beautiful, the family's accomplishment remarkable, and the guided tour of the little bakery and cannery in the old barn fascinating. The mill and store sell freshly ground, refrigerated flours, all kinds of freshly baked whole-grain breads and cookies, and a broad assortment of beans, nuts, grains, and cereals. The Keene family has won praise from such natural-food specialists as the authors of *Laurel's Kitchen* for producing wholesome food and maintaining a human scale in their successful operation. There are rest rooms, a lunch counter, a wooded picnic area close to Penns Creek, and all the untreated deep-well water you want.

You'll enjoy Walnut Acres more if you know a bit about the Keene family. Almost fifty years ago, Betty and Paul Keene started the project together. She was the daughter of a missionary in India; both she and Paul were teachers. They came to Pennsylvania with a baby and a small child, more or less broke, to live in an old (even then) farmhouse with no bathroom or furnace. The wood-and-coal cookstove heated the house. A single cold water faucet was the extent of their running water. Generations before the idea caught on, they determined to grow food without using poisons or chemicals on the soil, building the soil instead of simply feeding the plants quick fertilizer fixes. They thought that if they could grow plants sufficiently strong and healthy, in natural conditions, they wouldn't need insecticides because the plants would be naturally resistant to insects and disease. They kept track of how much the soil was improving by how soon the bugs began to leave. Paul recalls that it took them fifteen years to get everything in balance, but it worked. The farm prospered; the Keenes prospered; the business grew.

Today the Walnut Acres products are still processed by hand, vegetables such as peas are picked without machines, and tomatoes are peeled with knives instead of dipping in lye. Although their catalogs are now in full color and their order department computerized, the place still looks and operates like a family farm, with local folks contributing to the labor force. No matter how modern order fulfillment and shipping become, the farming doesn't change. In fifty years no fertilizers or chemicals have been used on the soil. Walk along the edge of a field. The soil is so friable you could almost work it with your hands. The difference is especially striking because commercial farming and canning operations throughout this part of the country have reduced some fields to gullied hardpan that have had to be put out of production and now stand fallow, mainly sprouting thistles.

Betty Keene, who'd lived for years longer than expected with an inherited disease, died recently. She worked in the office until a few days before her death. Some of the Keene children continue with the farm, as does Paul, who writes the catalog copy, including a long essay in each issue about our oneness with nature. The Globe Pequot Press has published a collection of these essays, *Fear Not to Sow Because of the Birds*. It's available through bookstores and at the farm.

If you find you have a taste for the Walnut Acres foods, you can continue eating them when you return home; they ship all over the country. Hours are Monday through Saturday 8:00 A.M. to 5:00 P.M., closed Sundays and holidays. Call (717) 837–0601. To get there, take Route 104 from Mifflinburg south to Penns Creek. Watch for a turnoff sign on the east side of Route 104 at the north end of the village. Walnut Acres is two minutes from that point.

Home of Little League

When you're done there, if the kids are with you, you might go back to Route 15 in Lewisburg and take the trip of about 30 miles north to Williamsport, home of Little League Baseball, to see the **Peter J. McGovern Little League Baseball Museum.** In addition to looking at the exhibits of uniforms, safety equipment, and Little League history and changes, the kids can bat and pitch in safety cages and then watch the instant replay on video monitors. In the theater the family can watch documentary films and old World Series games on film. They can test their knowledge on Little League and Major League rules at an electronic quiz board and also see and handle Little League equipment in various stages of production. Admission is $3.00 for adults, $1.00 for children, and $1.50 for senior citizens; the family rate is $8.00. The museum is open Memorial Day through Labor Day 10:00 A.M. to 8:00 P.M. and until 5:00 P.M. the rest of the year; Sunday hours are 1:00 P.M. to 5:00 P.M. It is closed Thanksgiving, Christmas, and New Year's Day. Call (717) 326–3607 for more information. The museum is on U.S. Route 15, 18 miles north of Interstate 80.

Another interesting stop in Williamsport is the Lycoming

County Historical Museum, displaying artifacts found locally that trace the stages of Indian culture from 10,000 years ago until the time of the first settlers. Other exhibits include a colonial kitchen, a quilting demonstration, a one-room school, the Indian Diorama of Bull Run Village, and a lumbering diorama. There is a gallery devoted to the history of lumbering in the area and an 1870s Victorian Parlor from "Millionaire Row." Millionaire Row in Williamsport dates back to when lumbering was a boom industry in Lycoming County, and Williamsport was the home of more millionaires per capita than any other city in the country. Also in the museum, the Shempp toy train collection, one of the finest toy train collections in the United States, consists of 337 complete trains and 100 individual locomotives. The trains are American Standard gauge, Early Standard gauge, and O gauge. Hours are Tuesday through Friday, 9:30 A.M. to 4:00 P.M., Sunday 1:30 P.M. to 4:00 P.M., and Saturday 9:30 A.M. to 4:00 P.M. and closed holidays. Admission is charged. The museum is at 858 West Fourth Street, and the phone number is (717) 326–3326.

If the glimpse of a millionaire's parlor whets your appetite for more, take the Millionaire's Row Tours, guided tours or walking tours of a row of mansions on West Fourth Street. Call the Lycoming County Tourist Agency to make arrangements or for more information (717–326–1971).

Then you can actually sit in a Victorian parlor of equal quality by spending the night at **Reighard House Bed and Breakfast Inn,** a brick and stone Victorian home with six guest rooms, all with private bath. The inn is the family home of Sue and Bill Reighard, who opened the bed and breakfast after retirement. The Eastlake furniture in the parlor has been in the family for four generations. No doubt you'll get a glimpse of Sue's humor. She is the kind of person who says, "I'm real good with corn flakes," while she's spreading a full country breakfast in front of you. The inn is at 1323 East Third Street, Williamsport (717–326–3593).

For dinner in yet another Victorian mansion, try the Peter Herdic House, at 407 West Fourth Street in Williamsport. The house is on the National Register of Historic Places, but, of course, you can't eat that. The menu is Continental, with fillets, chicken, and seafood among the favorites, and French pastries for dessert. It is open Monday through Friday 11:00 A.M. to midnight and Saturday 5:00 P.M. to midnight. Call (717) 322–0165 for information.

51

Wool Country

For people who like to shop in out-of-the-way places, the next logical move is west from Williamsport on Route 220 to Woolrich, to poke through **The Woolrich Store.** This is something like the L. L. Bean of Pennsylvania. Woolrich woolen fabrics, ready-to-wear clothing, and outdoor clothing are all for sale here at discount prices. Craftspeople may be interested in the bins of wool scraps for making braided rugs. The store is open 8:30 A.M. to 5:30 P.M. daily, to 9:00 P.M. Friday, and closed Sunday. The phone number is (717) 769–7401.

On the way to Woolrich, it's fun to take Route 287 north from Route 220, 4 miles to Salladasburg and **Cohick's Trading Post,** a general store selling groceries, hunting and fishing supplies, and famous homemade ice cream that even Katharine Hepburn has gone out of her way to taste. It is open from 7:00 A.M. to 10:00 P.M. daily; call (717) 398–0311.

Also on the way to Woolrich, it's fun to run through the little town of Hublersburg to get a taste of the kind of place that doesn't dress up for company because they don't expect any. It took the settlers of Hublersburg five tries to settle on a name. The place was first called Logan and was part of Lycoming County in 1829. About ten years later it became part of Centre County, and the name was changed to Hublersburgh. Three years later the name changed again, to Heckla. And three years after that, back to Hublersburgh. The *h* on the end of the name was typical of Pennsylvania spelling for all burghs at the time. Not until May 1893 did Hublersburg settle in with its current name. The official founding date is 1832.

The village is about 8 miles east of Pleasant Gap, on a short spur just south of Route 64. It has a population of a hundred or so people, with names like Dietrich and Heckman. Mostly older people live here. They spend time rolling old newspapers into logs to burn in their fireplaces and keeping track of who has the current honor of being the oldest in the community. Many of the old homes stand pretty much as they've always been, little modernized, certainly not self-consciously restored. It's the kind of drive that begs you to make up stories about the people and place as you pass through.

Central Pennsylvania Wineries

Kolin Vineyard
R.D. #1 Box 146
Bellefonte, PA 16823
(814) 355-4666

Nittany Valley Winery
724 South Athrton St.
State College, PA 16801
(814) 238-7562

Susquehanna Valley Winery
R.D. #5 Box 59
Danville, PA 17821
Phone not listed

Off the Beaten Path in North Central Pennsylvania

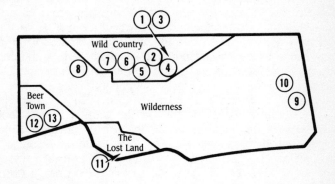

1. Pine Creek Gorge
2. Leonard Harrison State Park
3. Colton Point State Park
4. Penn Wells Hotel and Dining Room
5. The Log Cabin
6. Pennsylvania Lumber Museum
7. Susquehannock Trail
8. The Ice Mine
9. World's End State Park
10. Ricketts Glen State Park
11. Frenchville
12. Straub Brewery
13. Bucktail State Park

North Central Pennsylvania

Wild Country

A look at the map tells you a lot about the north central part of Pennsylvania. So does the common saying, "You really have to want to be there to get there, but it's worth the trip." From Williamsport, Route 15 goes north to Mansfield at Route 6. Or, from Route 220, between Williamsport and Jersey Shore, pick up Route 287 north to Wellsboro and Route 6. The area is mountainous and wooded, constituting mostly state parks, wilderness, and some slightly more civilized picnic areas. Unquestionably, the single most notable natural feature in the area is **Pine Creek Gorge,** more commonly known as the Grand Canyon of Pennsylvania. It is 50 miles long and 1,000 feet deep, covering 300,000 acres of state forest. There are two state parks, **Leonard Harrison** (phone 717–724–3061) on the east rim and **Colton Point** (717–724–3061) on the west, from where you can stop at many lookouts and pick up short hiking trails that don't require backpacking or safari gear. Leonard Harrison park has a good nature center and a relatively easy trail along the rim to give you an overall orientation to the canyon. More ambitious hikes that take in creeks and waterfalls are possible if you follow Turkey Path about a mile down to Pine Creek. The area is noted for a variety of ferns and songbirds. In Colton Point State Park you can pick up an easy mile-long loop to hike through a hardwood forest rich in astonishingly fragrant mountain laurel with its slightly sticky blooms, where you'll also find wild flowers. Most people visit the Grand Canyon of Pennsylvania in the fall for the foliage, but spring is really a nicer time, especially if you enjoy songbirds and wild flowers and like to avoid other tourists. The gorge is 10 miles west of Wellsboro on State Route 660.

To fully enjoy the area, it's a good idea to stop first in Wellsboro to get an area map from the Wellsboro State Chamber of Commerce, P.O. Box 733, 120 Main Street, Wellsboro 16901; phone (717) 724–1926.

Wellsboro is the Tioga County seat. It's a beautiful little town, with fine old trees and gaslights along the streets in the style of its New England founders from the beginning of the 1880s. You'll find more than a half dozen places to lodge there, ranging from well-rated motels such as the Penn Wells Motel on Main Street (717–724–3463), to the old **Penn Wells Hotel,** also on Main Street, where there's a pleasing old-style dining room, the **Penn Wells Dining Room,** that features a Saturday smorgasbord and a Sunday brunch, in addition to moderately priced luncheons and dinners. Cocktails are available. Call (717) 724–2111 for hotel and dining room. For casual dining, **The Log Cabin,** about 15 miles west on U.S. Route 6, is fun. Here you can dine casually on steaks or seafood, in the moderately high price range. Hours are 4:00 P.M. to 9:00 P.M., until 10:00 P.M. Friday and Saturday, and Sunday, noon to 9:00 P.M. Cocktails are available; call (814) 435–8808.

Also west of Wellsboro, on Route 6 across from Denton Hill State Park at Galeton, the **Pennsylvania Lumber Museum** depicts the history of Pennsylvania's prosperous lumbering activities a hundred years ago, when the white pine and hemlock in the woods were worth more than gold. The museum displays more than 3,000 artifacts related to the logging business, and the tour includes a walk among the old buildings of the logging camp and sawmill, all surrounded by Appalachian Mountain wilderness that makes the lumbering days feel very much alive. The complex includes Cook Shake, the mess and bunk halls, the sawmill, and a logging pond. The museum is open Tuesday through Saturday 9:00 A.M. to 5:00 P.M. and Sunday from noon to 5:00 P.M. Admission is charged; call (814) 435–2652 for details.

For hikers, the 85-mile **Susquehannock Trail** can be entered here, as can countless marked trails in the state forests.

Wilderness

Farther away, about 50 miles west of Wellsboro, still on Route 6, in the little town of Coudersport, population less than 3,000, you can visit **The Ice Mine,** a phenomenon of nature where the hotter the weather, the more ice forms, while in the coldest part of winter there's no ice at all. At Coudersport, take Route 44 a few miles north to the mine.

Two other near-wilderness parks that you really have to want to get to, equally worth the time, are **World's End State Park** and **Ricketts Glen State Park,** in the northern tier of central

Pennsylvania. Part of the fun of World's End is its high elevation and primitive quality. It is not on any major road. Once you leave Route 220, going west on Route 154 will get you there. It's a good place for picnicking, fishing, swimming, and boating. Cabins are available for rental. They are very rustic. You may prefer to stay in one of the boarding houses or tourist homes in the nearby town of Eagles Mere, where you'll also find a number of simple eating places. The park phone number is (717) 924–3287.

Ricketts Glen is considered by knowledgeable outdoorsmen and women to be the most spectacular of Pennsylvania's state parks. Its more than 13,000 acres of mountains, streams, water-falls, and lakes spread through Sullivan, Columbia, and Luzerne counties. There are twenty-three named waterfalls, a virgin hem-lock forest in which many of the trees are more than 500 years old, a number of trout pools in Kitchen Creek, and bass in Lake Jean. You'll also find a beach for swimming on this lake. The park has 20 miles of hiking trails, some strictly for the physically fit and some shorter loops that are less strenuous. One trail along the gorge gives you a view of many waterfalls and is breathtak-ingly close to the edge. Astonishingly, except for locals, relatively few people know about the park or visit it. It is possible to find deserted hiking trails almost any time and wander into the woods feeling like the only person in the forest primeval. In more cleared areas, food is available. Cabins are available for rental and the park has good camping for recreational vehicles (if you don't mind driving one up such steep roads) and tenters. To get there, the least arduous way is to take Route 487 from Route 220 at Dushore to Lake Jean. The park phone number is (717) 477–5675.

The Lost Land

Going to **Frenchville** can't be an afterthought; you have to make up your mind to make the trip. No place in Pennsylvania could care less about enticing tourists. In fact, little more than twenty years ago, researchers going there preferred to travel in pairs. The little village of several hundred people hides in a pocket of hills in the mountainous area of Clearfield County, near no major city and no important landmark. Your drive takes you through the kind of countryside that science fiction movie producers look for to film prehistoric earth. The trip over pitted blacktop roads winds through the remains of played-out strip mines, some of them growing scraggly conifers planted as part of reclamation projects. The few outsiders who venture to Frenchville come because of the language. People in Frenchville speak a classically pure French, without any American accent and without the slang of contemporary French streets. Hardly a generation ago, most of the adults could not read or write French. Even the inscriptions on tombstones are misspelled and grammatically incorrect. But the people *speak* French flawlessly.

What seems to have happened begins nearly 150 years ago, when the villagers' French ancestors walked overland from parts of Baltimore and New York to settle here. Apparently they walked because when they signed their purchase agreements for what seemed like bargain terms (twelve acres free with each fifty bought), they didn't understand that they were making a deal for isolated land inaccessible by normal transport. In this isolation, the men farmed, mined, worked on nearby railroads as they developed, and stuck together, speaking French among themselves. Outside the community they spoke a little English, but since nobody got into extended conversations with foreign miners and railroad workers, it didn't add up to much. As new inventions came along, the villagers simply incorporated English words for them into their talk—*automobile, radio, television.* Aside from such words, the language in Frenchville remained pure, classical French.

Consolidated schools educating children outside the community have been diluting the effect for the past ten or twenty years, as has television, but you can hear the old speech still, from villagers named Roussey, Rogeux, Habovick, and Plubell, people who remember apple-butter-making parties and village festivals. The best way to get a taste of the phenomenon and of a special village is to park your car, walk the streets, wander through the graveyard inspecting headstones, stop into the few stores, the tavern, and perhaps the post office, and simply, respectfully, listen. To get to Frenchville, go north on Route 879 from Interstate 80 at Clearfield. After your visit to the town, you may want to return to Clearfield, where you'll find fairly inexpensive rates at any one of several good quality standard motels. You may enjoy walking the Clearfield streets to see several historic buildings that are still in full use downtown.

Beertown

Not near anything else in this northern tier, at an altitude of 1,702 feet, the little city of St. Marys has one major claim to fame in the eyes of Pennsylvanians—**Straub Brewery,** at 303 Sorg Street. Straub's is one of the smallest independent breweries left in the United States. They produce a beer (made only of water, malt, grains, and hops, with no sugar syrups or additives of any kind) that people who love beer rank above any American and most imported beer. The company distributes only within a radius of 150 miles, which means to get the beer you either have to be in the area or entice a friend from the area to visit you bearing gifts. For people who value the quality, taste, and individuality of a pure beer brewed in a tiny brewery, it's worth a drive to tour the plant and stock up. St. Marys is where Routes 255 and 120 intersect, between Ridgeway and Emporium. Hours are Monday through Friday, 9:00 A.M. to noon, for free tours and tastings. The brewery is closed holidays. Call (814) 834-2875.

From Emporium, the 23,013-acre **Bucktail State Park** extends down along the Susquehanna River southeast to Lockhaven. State Route 120, a good road between the mountains, makes this a pleasant, scenic drive through some of the wildest country in Pennsylvania, because Bucktail is surrounded by more state forests and parks, wild areas, and natural areas, but if you're in the mood for a more active experience, the place is full of hiking trails and clearings where you can enjoy the view and a picnic. You can count on being alone here. Incidentally, the park's name comes only indirectly from the deer of the same name; the park commemorates a regiment of woodsmen from the area who called themselves the Bucktail Regiment when they served in the Civil War.

North Central Pennsylvania Wineries

Brookmere Farm Vineyards
Rt. 655
Bellville, PA 17004
(717) 935-5380

Oak Springs Winery
R.D. #2 Box 604
Altoona, PA 16601
(814) 946-3799

Oregon Hill Winery
R.D. #1
Morris, PA 16938
(717) 353-2711

Off the Beaten Path in South Central Pennsylvania

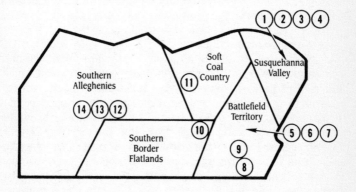

1. Millersburg Ferry
2. Katy's Kitchen and Tea Room
3. Perry County
4. Duncannon
5. Gettysburg National Military Park
6. A. Lincoln's Place
7. Eisenhower National Historic Site
8. Historic Fairfield Inn
9. Hickory Bridge Farm
10. Chambersburg Volunteer Fireman's Museum
11. East Broad Top Railroad
12. Espy House
13. Old Bedford Village
14. Jean Bonnet Tavern

South Central Pennsylvania

Susquehanna Valley

Most people driving along the Susquehanna River between Sunbury and Harrisburg take Routes 11 and 15 on the west side of the river for speed, but on the east side, the less-traveled Route 147 gives you some lovely glimpses of the river valley and the tiny, interesting river towns that dot the shores. In Millersburg, the **Millersburg Ferry,** the only surviving ferry on the Susquehanna, still runs a mile back and forth at one of the widest points of the Susquehanna, connecting Millersburg with Perry County near Liverpool. A Historic Site Landmark, the ferry first went into operation in 1825, an improvement for passengers and freight haulers over the rowboats and pole boats they'd been using. At the peak of river commerce, four boats made the trips. Now only the Falcon and Roaring Bull, heated by wood stoves in winter, remain, and it's a pretty casual operation. A rough sign lettered on four boards nailed horizontally to a post says: FERRY IS RUNNING/DRIVE DOWN THE HILL/AND I'LL COME/AND GET YOU. You sort of have to guess when, knowing that the trip, one way, takes about twenty minutes. Each ferry boat accommodates four cars and sixty passengers. Without your car you could almost wade the mile; the river at this crossing rarely goes more than 3 feet deep. The ferry may stop operating soon, but it's worth trying for as long as possible. Moreover, your business could be the added impetus needed to keep it running. To find the pick-up point, drive into Millersburg on Route 147 and follow signs to the crossing site. Call (717) 444–3200 for more information.

While you're in Millersburg, wander through the historic section to see the old buildings, then run over to 107 Market Street for a bite to eat in **Katy's Kitchen and Tea Room.** The restaurant building used to be the Auchmuty House, built by Samuel Auchmuty in about 1868 and inhabited by his eccentric daughters, Annie and Eugenie, who stuffed the upstairs back rooms to the ceiling with isinglass containers and kept money under the floorboards in the bedroom. The isinglass containers are gone, and no doubt the money is too, but the rooms downstairs are still

quaint, if not eccentric, with all kinds of handmade country collectibles that are for sale crammed on the shelves of antique
cupboards. The tearoom is known for its cran-apple tea and an
assortment of soups, salads, and sandwiches and Mud Pie for
dessert. It is open Tuesday through Saturday, 11:00 A.M. to 2:00
P.M.; call (717) 692–4543.

Whether you cross on the ferry or drive south to the bridge at
Clarks Ferry, eventually you'll want to get to the other side to
explore **Perry County.** At Liverpool, just off Routes 11 and 15,
across from the ferry landing, Hunters Valley Winery, on a 150-
year-old farm in the valley, combines traditional wine-making
methods with such new technology as stainless steel fermenters
and fine filtration to produce their wines. Their grapes come from
vineyards planted on the high slopes overlooking the Susquehanna River in 1982. In many ways the growing conditions resemble those in parts of France, with full sun, good air
circulation, excellent water drainage, and temperatures moder-
ated by the river and mountains. Visitors may walk through the
vineyards and picnic on the grounds. The winery is open Friday
from 1:00 P.M. to 7:00 P.M. and Saturday and Sunday from 11:00
A.M. to 5:00 P.M. Call (717) 564–8177.

South of Liverpool, still on Routes 11 and 15, drive through
Duncannon, a little railroad and river town featured a few years
ago in *National Geographic* for its continuing sense of working
class neighborhood rather than for being picturesque. In Duncannon, people still borrow a cup of sugar, bring food when someone
in the family dies, and talk about what's happening at church.
Because of its proximity to the Appalachian Trail, it's become a
rest spot for hikers, who usually stay at the old Hotel Doyle, on
Market Square. You'll find several eating places, including a diner,
in and around Duncannon. Stop at least for coffee to give yourself a chance to listen to the local talk.

Elsewhere in Perry County, you could drive for a couple of
days, through about 550 square miles, trying to take in all the
historic and natural attractions—fourteen covered bridges,
twenty-four old mills, twenty-seven historical locations, fourteen
hiking trails passing through, ten scenic overlooks, three national
natural landmarks, six rural parks, and a partridgeberry tree.
Write for a booklet listing and showing locations of all the attractions as well as hotels and eating places: Perry Tourist Bureau,
Box 447, New Bloomfield, PA 17068 (717–834–4912). Ask for

their literature even if you can't go there. These people formed a volunteer tourist bureau producing booklets and brochures worthy of special mention. They'll tell you that in 1980 one of their holstein herds produced the highest milk and butterfat ratings in the state on a per-cow basis; their chickens laid an average of 262 eggs per bird, and their cornfields yielded sixty bushels of corn per acre, all for total production running up to eight digits. They print older folks' recollections of a father who raced the train on his bicycle while the passengers cheered, laundry baskets and washtubs full of food hauled to annual picnics, and fiddlers who picked up the tempo to keep dancers hopping. Also, they sell appealing prints of historic landmarks in Perry County done by local artist Scotty Brown. The prints have appeared in the publicity and history brochures. What an antidote to airbrushed color photos emblazoned with screaming headlines and printed on fifty-pound glossy paper! Pure Pennsylvania.

Battlefield Territory

You shouldn't miss Gettysburg, where the Yankee and Confederate soldiers fought the bloodiest battle of the Civil War in 1863. Admittedly, the area is slickly organized for tourism, but the history is well and interestingly communicated, and the area feels more rural than urban. **Gettysburg National Military Park** surrounds the city of Gettysburg. The visitor center is across from the entrance on State Route 134. Battlefield tours start from here, and exhibits explain the battle. The most dramatic exhibit, in Cyclorama Center, complete with a sound and light show, centers around Paul Philippoteaux's famous 1884 painting, *Pickett's Charge*. Elsewhere, in the center, displays of Civil War weapons and uniforms complete the picture. Because the battlefield is 6 miles by 7 miles, you may want to take a bus tour with the Gettysburg Tour Center. A stereo narration recreates the Battle of Gettysburg as the double-decker bus crosses the battlefield. The tour takes about two hours. The center (714–334–6245) provides free shuttle service to and from all major motels and campgrounds.

At least two dozen attractions related to the Battle of Gettysburg and the Civil War clamor for your attention, including The National Civil War Wax Museum (717–334–6245), the Jennie

Wade House and Olde Town (717–334–4100), and Gettysburg Battle Theatre (717–334–6100). For a complete listing of attractions, dining, camping, and lodging, write Gettysburg Travel Council, 35 Carlisle Street, Gettysburg, PA 17325, or call (717) 334–6274.

In one form or another, try to catch a live performance of James A. Getty as Abraham Lincoln. For more than a decade, Getty and his wife, Joanne, have run **A. Lincoln's Place,** a multi-faceted business centered around his forty-minute performances as Lincoln. The shows trace Lincoln's life from his boyhood in Kentucky through his presidency. The Gettys came from Illinois, naturally knowing a little something about Lincoln, but James was a choral conductor, neither an actor nor a historian. Then he grew a beard and, Mrs. Getty says, "The beard made him do it." Getty immersed himself in research about Abraham Lincoln and then began his performances. "Now we know a *lot* about Lincoln," Joanne Getty says. James tailors his shows to the age level of his audience, changing them as his continuing research turns up new information. He performed at both at the A. Lincoln Place Theatre in Gettysburg, where Mrs. Getty managed the theater and its gift shop, and on tour. James's shows won the Pennsylvania Travel Excellence Award. The theater has just closed because James and Joanne couldn't keep up the pace any longer and because he'd become too busy to maintain his research. But the touring performances will continue, as will local performances at The Conflict Theatre, 213 Steinwehr Avenue (717–334–8003). At the time of this writing Getty's performances are scheduled for 8:00 P.M. Monday through Thursday in the summer, but these hours and possibly even the location could change. He almost certainly will perform at other places and times in Gettysburg, probably several times a day, as ever. The telephone for A. Lincoln's Place will ring, as it always has, in the Getty's home (717–334–6049). Call to learn where you can see a show before you visit the area. A performance by a man whose beard led him to study and portray Lincoln and whose passion makes him keep a business phone at home embodies the very spirit of this book.

Also at Gettysburg, the **Eisenhower National Historic Site** recalls and commemorates Ike's presidential and military years. The easiest way to get there is on a shuttle bus from the National Park Visitor Center. The site, open to the public, includes the Eisenhower 230-acre farm and farmhouse, the only home they ever owned; a putting green and sandtrap once given to the president by the Professional Golfer's Association; and a brick barbecue grill where Ike broiled 3-inch-thick steaks for guests. Eisenhower's shooting range, cattle barn, and the milk house where the Secret Service office was ensconced are not open to the public yet. The home was not opened to the public until 1980, shortly after Mamie died. Visitors find the farmhouse homey rather than grand, not really decorated, but rather simply furnished almost entirely with gifts showered on the Eisenhowers during his forty-five years of national service. On the glassed-in porch where the couple preferred to spend their time stands an unfinished painting by Ike. He completed at least 260 others during the last twenty years of his life. A few of them hang in the house.

Eisenhower said he could get a better sense of what a person was truly about by entertaining him at home. Guests included Nikita Krushchev, Charles De Gaulle, and Winston Churchill. Visiting here brings the presidency and world figures into an uncommonly human focus. There is a modest admission charge. The hours and the number of visitors allowed vary—call first (717–334–1124).

To dine and bed down in the spirit of Gettysburg's history and Eisenhower's farm, consider the **Historic Fairfield Inn** or **Hickory Bridge Farm,** both only about ten or twenty minutes from the battlefield. At the Historic Fairfield Inn, in the village of Fairfield, you stay in one of six guest rooms, all with shared bath, in the plantation home of Squire William Miller, who laid out the town in 1801. The building became an inn in 1823. Country cooking is the big attraction here—crab cakes or chicken and biscuits, lots of vegetables, and homemade fruit cobblers with ice cream. The inn and restaurant close from time to time for holidays and vacations. Make plans and reservations well ahead of time. Call (717) 642–5410. Hickory Bridge Inn, in Ortanna, run by Nancy Jean Hammett and Mary Lou Martin, offers seven rooms, including cottages, with private bath. It's a genuine farmstead with a red barn turned restaurant, a country museum with old farm equipment, a pond, and a trout stream, surrounded by fifty acres of farm land. Literature about the place claims that guests swim in the spring-fed pond in summer, but anyone who's ever stuck a foot into spring water at the source will take that information skeptically. The rooms are quiet, furnished with Pennsylvania Dutch items and antiques, and the cottages have wood-burning stoves. In the restaurant you're offered amazing quantities of Pennsylvania Dutch cooking in a designer-country setting. The inn is closed from just before Christmas until the first of the new year. Call (717) 642–5261 for more information.

Southern Border Flatlands

More Civil War history waits at Chambersburg, the next major stop on Route 30 west after Gettysburg. In the 1960s, Chambersburg won recognition, along with several other smaller Pennsylvania cities, for early efforts to preserve historic areas as part of city development plans. While the city could claim much history, actual historic buildings were in such short supply that saving them seemed especially important because the Confederates occupied the city three times during the Civil War. The last time, in 1864, 3,000 Confederate soldiers rode into town demanding $100,000 ransom in gold. Chambersburg couldn't pay; the Confederates burned the town, putting two thirds of its citizenry out of homes. Then the raiders rode off to McConnellsburg. Mention it the next time someone talks about Sherman burning Atlanta. Pick up a brochure with a mapped walking tour of downtown Chambersburg at the chamber of commerce, 75 South Second Street. Either appropriately or ironically, the museum of note here is the **Chambersburg Volunteer Fireman's Museum,** 441 Broad Street. In the original firehouse, the museum exhibits trucks, pumpers, a steamer, and other equipment from the nineteenth century. The museum is open summers from 1:00 P.M. to 9:00 P.M. Saturday and to 5:00 P.M. Sunday; winter hours are by appointment. Donations are accepted for admission. Call (717) 263–1049.

Soft Coal Country

Head on toward McConnellsburg, on the heels of the Rebel warriors, to pick up Route 522 north, crossing the Pennsylvania Turnpike and continuing north to the **East Broad Top Railroad,** a Registered National Historic Landmark at Orbisonia. Some railroad buffs will certainly argue that East Broad Top is the best train attraction in Pennsylvania. It is the last 3-foot gauge

East Broad Top Railroad

(narrow gauge) line in the east still operating from its original site. It was built in 1873 to move coal from the bituminous coal mines of central Pennsylvania to Mt. Union, where the coal was dumped into standard gauge cars on the Pennsylvania Railroad. The EBT hauled coal until 1956! Today the train runs a 10-mile trip that takes almost an hour, hauling mostly nuts—the people kind, not the tree kind. Not only does the EBT attract railroad enthusiasts, it also calls to photographers and sound-recording nuts. Crazy guys with absolutely top quality recording equipment show up every so often, lugging Nagra tape recorders and stringing microphones all along the track to record the Doppler effect or to try to get the chuggs and choos of the train's coming and going recorded in stereo to pick up background sounds for a film or media show.

For just plain folks, the ride is scenic, fun, and educational. In the roundhouse you can still look over several steam locomotives and puzzle over the M-1 gas electric car built in the mid-1920s with help from Westinghouse at EBT shops. Complete picnic facilities are available the end of the line. Often folks stop there and come back on a later train. All up and down the line, you can either be a nut or watch the nuts. It's a plain good time. Trains leave on the hour from 11:00 A.M. to 4:00 P.M. weekends in June, September, and October and daily in July and August. Rates are moderate. Write EBT Railroad, Rockhill Furnace, PA 17249 or call (814) 447–3011.

Southern Alleghenies

Going to Orbisonia will have taken you off Route 30. At this point you can either head to the center of the state on Routes 22 and 322 to arrive in State College or to drive east to Harrisburg, or you can backtrack briefly on either the Pennsylvania Turnpike (not recommended) or Route 30 to Bedford and Bedford Springs in the Allegheny Mountain area. Settlement here goes back to 1751. Much of the area's history is preserved in restored and reconstructed buildings. In the historic district, start at the visitor information center at 137 East Pitt Street, open Monday through Friday (and Saturdays June through October) 8:30 A.M. to 4:30 P.M. Phone (814) 623–1771. Pick up a map and information for a self-guided tour that will include at least thirteen sites. One of these,

Espy House, dating back to the late 1700s, served as the headquarters of George Washington when 13,000 troops came here to put down the rebellion of citizens in the "Whiskey Belt" against an excise tax on whiskey—the 1794 Whiskey Rebellion.

At another stop, you can still see the trenches by the road where in 1863 troops dug in against Confederate soldiers expected to attack the railroad at Altoona. The rebels marched toward Gettysburg instead, making the trenches unnecessary. At Bedford Springs, President James Buchanan came to take the healing waters and made the springs his summer White House.

Old Bedford Village recreates Pennsylvania pioneer life, with more than forty log homes and craft shops, one-room schools, and other buildings brought from different places and rebuilt here, reproducing a colonial village. More interesting than the buildings, costumed guides and artisans demonstrate an unusually large variety of early skills and crafts—potting, making brooms, cooking, weaving baskets, tanning hides, even firing long rifles. The activities sprawl over seventy-two acres, though of course all the land is not used for buildings. But it's a lot of walking; the tour takes three hours. Old Bedford Village accommodates people in wheelchairs. Sometimes a tour of this length tempts kids to try to hitch a ride; sometimes gracious people let them. Bedford Village is open 9:00 A.M. to 5:00 P.M. daily. Old Bedford Village schedules an almost continuous string of special festivals and demonstrations. Write for further information: P.O. Box 1976, Bedford, PA 15522 (814–623–1156). Moderate admission is charged.

At the **Jean Bonnet Tavern,** one of the oldest taverns in western Pennsylvania (circa 1762), 4 miles west of Bedford on Route 30, try a steak dinner, the tavern's specialty. The dining room and tavern areas are separate and are open daily, 11:00 A.M. to 10:00 P.M. Call (814) 623–2250.

If you keep going west on Route 30, Coral Caverns, 7 miles from Bedford, offers tours of the only known coral reef caverns, formed more than 300 million years ago while the area was still covered by the Appalachian Sea. Open Memorial Day to Labor Day, 10:00 A.M. to 6:00 P.M., weekends only the rest of the year. Admission prices are moderate. Call (814) 623–6882 for details.

Off the Beaten Path in Northeastern Pennsylvania

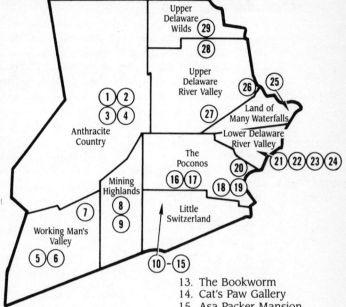

1. Scranton Iron Furnaces
2. Steamtown Historic Site
3. Pennsylvania Anthracite Museum
4. McDade Park
5. Anthracite Museum at Ashland
6. Pioneer Coal Mine Tunnel
7. Genetti's Motor Lodge, Dinner Playhouse & Conference Center
8. Beacon Diner
9. Nesquahoning
10. Jim Thorpe Mausoleum
11. Jim Thorpe Railroad Station
12. Old Mauch Chunk Scale Model Railroad HO Display
13. The Bookworm
14. Cat's Paw Gallery
15. Asa Packer Mansion
16. Trainers Inn
17. New Apollo Restaurant
18. The Inn at Kresgeville
19. Cherry Valley Vineyards
20. Quiet Valley Living Historical Farm
21. Delaware Water Gap
22. Mary Stolz Doll and Toy Museum
23. The Pocono Indian Museum
24. The Craft Gallery of Pennsylvania Designer Craftsmen
25. Bushkill Falls
26. Swiss Country Inn
27. Sterling Inn
28. Settler's Inn
29. Sylvania Tree Farm

Northeastern Pennsylvania

Anthracite Country

To understand eastern Pennsylvania, you need to understand coal mining. The anthracite coal region of eastern Pennsylvania is not particularly pretty. Although some stretches of highway through the hills are lovely, much of the landscape has been marred by the coal-mining operations that used to be the economic mainstay of the region. Nor can the working mines be called aesthetically pleasing by any usual standard. But the area is historically rich, not with battle sites or great government buildings, but in the details that let us see how people there used to live and work. Nowhere is this more obvious than in Scranton, where coal and iron were at their peak until the end of World War II, when the demand for coal diminished. In downtown Scranton, on Cedar Avenue, between Lackawanna Avenue and Moosic Street, the **Scranton Iron Furnaces** are open daily from 8:00 A.M. to dusk. These four huge blast furnace stacks, built between 1841 and 1857, are the remnants of the iron industry around which Scranton grew, with coal mining and railroads falling into place as companion industries. Admission is free; call (717) 963–4804.

Emphasizing the relationship between iron, railroads, and coal, within walking distance of the iron furnaces, is a terminal at Lackawanna Station for the **Steamtown Historic Site,** a working steam railroad on which you can take a scenic ride from Scranton to Moscow, about 12 miles south, and back. As this was written, the schedules were not definite because the operation had just been taken over by the National Park Service. The fare is moderate; call (717) 343–0760.

Continue your education by going through the **Pennsylvania Anthracite Museum,** which features exhibits related to the lives and work of the ethnic communities in the region. Exhibits survey activities related to canals, railroads, silk mills, and factories, and, of course, coal. The museum is on Bald Mountain Road in Dade Park. Take the North Scranton Expressway to the Keyser Avenue exit. Follow Keyser Avenue and the signs to McDade Park.

The museum is open 9:00 A.M. to 5:00 P.M. Monday through Saturday, from noon to 5:00 P.M. Sunday. Admission is $2.00 for adults, $1.50 for senior citizens, and $1 for children. Call (717) 963–4804.

McDade Park has picnic tables and charcoal burners if you'd like to snatch a bite before going on to the Lackawanna Coal Mine Tour, which begins next to the museum. This tour takes you down into an actual abandoned slope mine to see what the miners did and what conditions were like there. Tourists are lowered from the loading platform to the mine interior in an electrically hoisted car. The big yellow iron car and hoist are new and were designed especially for this purpose, so you need not worry that you'll be in an old creaking car of the sort you've seen in old movies. Inside the mine, a tour guide, either a retired miner or a teacher who's been trained by a retired miner, will take you on a 600-foot walking tour on a wooden walkway, explaining what you see and answering questions. The underground area is spacious; even claustrophobic visitors shouldn't feel closed in. Mannequins in mining clothes and a life-sized stuffed mule add verisimilitude. Although the mine isn't really dirty, it is underground, and coal can leave its marks, so consider this a blue-jeans-and-walking-shoes excursion. The tours last about an hour. New tours leave hourly, more frequently during busy times. More exhibits and artifacts are housed above ground in a new addition to the building called Shifting Shanty. From May through October, tours begin at 11:00 A.M.; the last tour starts at 4:30 P.M. Phone (717) 963–6463.

Working Men's Valleys

From Scranton you can get to Hazelton quickly on Interstate 81, or cross over to Route 11 and drive down along the Susquehanna for a while to see some of the little river towns. These are not the picturesque, renovated towns of slick decorating magazines, but real, working towns inhabited by Pennsylvania's laboring folks. Driving through here you may still see women wearing babushkas (head scarves), kids scuffing their shoes on the sidewalks, and town merchants sitting in front of their stores during idle moments. From about Wilkes Barre, the drive becomes especially mountainous in the narrow river valley, giving you the sensation that the mountains are close around your ears. Almost any time you tire of it, you can pick up a short road back to the interstate to Hazleton, another coal town that has now moved into other kinds of industry to compensate for the spent mines and the declining demand for coal. Here, Eckley Miners' Village gives you a chance to visit a spot that is part historic site and part living community. It is authentic, not because it has been recreated, but because it never changed. How could one recreate the black silt heaps and open strip mines and slag left from earlier operations surrounding the village? It was a company town from its settlement in 1854 until 1971. Now it's administered by the Pennsylvania Historical and Museum Commission, but more than fifty people, retired miners, their widows, and children, still live here. The village, covering one hundred acres, includes fifty-eight buildings and exhibits showing what daily life was like for coal-mining families. These people were the ethnic groups of immigrants who found their work in the coal fields: first English, Welsh, and Germans, then Irish and Eastern Europeans. The village is 9 miles east of Hazleton, off State Route 940. Follow signs to the site, which is open Monday through Saturday from 9:00 A.M. to 5:00 P.M. and from noon to 5:00 P.M. on Sunday. It is closed holidays, except Memorial Day, July 4, and Labor Day. A modest admission fee is charged. Call (717) 636–2070.

Another interesting pair of stops in the vicinity is the **Anthracite Museum at Ashland** and **Pioneer Coal Mine Tunnel,** on State Route 61, off Interstate 81 about 20 miles south of Hazleton. Pioneer Coal Mine is the first mine to have been opened to the public and has been operated as a nonprofit community project for more than twenty-five years. It is a drift mine tunnelled almost horizontally a half-mile into Mahanoy Mountain about 450 feet down. Pioneer Tunnel follows an anthracite vein that is nearly 200 feet thick in some places. The miners who worked in it before it was blasted shut to close it down in 1931 were able to work standing up. In mines with thinner seams, miners had to work on their knees. The tour, in a small train pulled by a little locomotive powered with batteries, begins at the entrance of the mine and passes the big vein, where you can see the tunnels branching off the main tunnel. It takes about a half hour. To see an open pit mine that was dug close to the surface with steam shovels, and a "bootleg hole" where poachers dug out coal, take the steam engine "Lokie" for its half-hour tour around Mahanoy Mountain—on the outside, not through tunnels. To get to Pioneer Coal Mine, take Route 61 into Ashland, where it becomes Center Street. Turn left (south) on 19th Street and continue for three blocks. The mine is open from Memorial Day to Labor Day from 10:00 A.M. to 6:00 P.M. daily, weekends only from Labor Day to October 31. A moderate admission fee is charged. Call (717) 875–3850 for more information.

One street over, the Anthracite Museum on 18th Street features a collection of tools, machinery, and photographs showing how hard coal has been mined from the early pick-and-shovel days to contemporary surface mining operations. The museum is open from Memorial Day to Labor Day, 10:00 A.M. to 6:00 P.M., Monday through Saturday and noon to 6:00 P.M. Sunday. The rest of the year, hours are 9:00 A.M. to 5:00 P.M. Tuesday through Saturday and noon to 5:00 P.M. Sunday. Admission is modest. Call (717) 875–4708.

An entertaining way to get a fuller sense of the character of the area today, as it has grown from its earlier roots, is to eat or spend the night at **Genetti's Motor Lodge, Dinner Playhouse & Conference Center,** on Route 309 at Hazleton. This good-sized operation dates back several decades to its beginnings as Gus Genetti's popular Italian restaurant in pre-interstate days, when Route 301 was a major highway. Gus was widely known for always having lots of different projects going, including, at one time, a mink ranch behind the restaurant. Gus is dead now, the mink ranch gone, but the Genetti family continues in that same eclectic spirit.

Genetti's is a Best Western, but Best Westerns are independently owned, and no franchise sameness marks this one. The complex sprawls from near the highway, close to where the original restaurant stood, back down a hill and into the northern suburbs of Hazelton. From the parking lots behind some of the units you can see kids playing at the swings and sandboxes of their grassy backyards. In addition to the lodge rooms, three restaurants of varying degrees of formality offer Italian specialties along with more standard fare and a dinner theater features performers ranging from the Lettermen and Blackstone, the magician, to performances of Broadway musicals and light comedy plays. There's also a swimming pool and a pleasant patio. The rooms are luxuriously appointed, mainly with oak and cherry furniture and king-sized beds.

It's a bonus that the people who work here are local, mostly from families that have been in the area for generations, and can tell you lots about Hazleton and the colorful Gus Genetti.

Obviously, with so much going on, this is not a quiet hideaway, especially on weekends, but often on nights early in the week, business is slow and the place is calm. Because of the additional activity that comes with dinner theater performances and conferences, reservations are important even during slow seasons, both to make sure you can get in and to let you know in advance what's going to be happening. The lodge phone number is (717) 454–2494; the dinner playhouse phone number is (717) 455–3691.

Mining Highlands

If you're looking for an authentic view of northeastern Pennsylvania, not embellished by brochure prose or photographs, try this slightly circuitous drive from Hazelton to historic Jim Thorpe to get a sense of (and participate in) the real day-to-day workings of the area. Take Route 309 from Hazelton south toward Tamaqua. You'll drive through mountain sections that alternately astonish you with their beauty and dismay you with the way that the beauty is marred by the accoutrements of producing, shipping, and using coal—silt, slag, smokestacks, tipples, trucks, and tracks, all seeming anomalies in the landscape, but inevitable in the process. Here and there a tree will grow defiantly out of the slag. In a few miles, at the intersection of Route 309 and Route 54, stop at the **Beacon Diner,** a real old-time diner, silver on the outside, with swivel seats at the counter and booths along the windows. You can order from standard menu choices of sandwiches, specials, fries, and the like, but a better treat is a big, fat, round sticky bun with good coffee or a milkshake made in an honest-to-goodness milkshake mixer from real ice cream and milk. If you sit at the counter, you can joke with the waitresses about whether or not sticky buns are allowed by Weight Watchers and eavesdrop a bit to pick up current local small talk.

After refreshment, take Route 54 east through **Nesquahoning,** a little mining town built on hills so steep that nothing seems level. Businesses and homes share the same streets. Driving slowly, you can peek through a barbershop window to glimpse an elderly gentleman getting a haircut while he chats with cronies. In front of the homes, flourishing flowers spill from their beds over cement walls toward the sidewalk. Occasionally a dog threatens a shrub and scampers away when he's reprimanded with a rolled newspaper. In backyards, women in jeans or cotton housedresses hang laundry to dry on clotheslines. Then you're through town, and signs lead you down the mountain into Jim Thorpe.

Little Switzerland

If anybody had told the old-timers that one day Mauch Chunk (pronounced *maw-chunk*) would be named Jim Thorpe in honor of an American Indian Olympic athlete and football player from Oklahoma, who was buried here even though he'd never lived here, they'd have smiled. If anybody had said that Mauch Chunk would become a tourist attraction and that the best-selling books in town would be about restoring Victorian homes, the old-timers would have guffawed. Until about 1950, Mauch Chunk was another Pennsylvania mining town whose economy fluctuated with the coal market, where miners lived in uncertainty, and millionaires lived in mansions. Trying to survive, citizens of Mauch Chunk and East Mauch Chunk were donating a nickel a week to an economic development fund. Meanwhile, Jim Thorpe's wife was looking for a way to right a series of insults that had been heaped upon her husband before he died. In 1912 he had won two gold medals and broken many pentathlon and decathlon records to become a hero at the Olympic games in Stockholm. But when the Olympic committee discovered that he had played one season of professional baseball for $60 a month, they stripped him of all his awards because he was not an amateur. After he died of cancer, penniless, Oklahoma refused to build him a monument, so his wife started looking for a place where he could be buried with honor. Admiring the fighting spirit of Mauch Chunk and East Mauch Chunk, she approached the two towns with her idea. The towns incorporated to become Jim Thorpe and erected a large granite mausoleum on the east side of town. On the tombstone, read the words of King Gustav of Sweden when he presented the Olympic Medals to Thorpe in 1912: "Sir, you are the greatest athlete in the world." The monument was never turned into a honky-tonk tourist attraction, but the publicity that came to the town as a result of the change combined with the cooperation between what had been two rival communities helped turn the economy here around. In a posthumous reversal, Thorpe's amateur status was reinstated in 1982. A year later the committee presented replicas of his gold medals to his family. **The Jim Thorpe Mausoleum** is $1/2$ mile east of Jim Thorpe on Route 903.

Another interesting site, this one overlooking Route 209 at the base of Mount Pisgah, is a memorial plaque where the village of Northern Liberties used to be. In 1861 virtually all the village men and boys between the ages of 16 and 26 volunteered to serve the Union in the Civil War, effectively destroying the village by killing off its reproductive population. All that remains is the plaque memorializing the soldiers, attached to a large rock where the village used to stand.

More lighthearted history awaits in the heart of downtown Jim Thorpe. After you drive down the mountain into town, park in one of the public lots or at one of the meters where you still get an hour for a dime to explore the narrow, winding streets on foot. This area at the foot of the hills is Hazard Square. It quickly becomes obvious how it got its name. Drive defensively and walk across the streets as if you were in a war zone. At the center of all this, in the **Jim Thorpe Railroad Station,** you can buy tickets for rides on steam locomotive trains through the mountains to Nesquahoning and back, an 8-mile round trip, in the spring and summer. During the autumn foliage season, longer trips of nearly three hours to Haucks and back leave twice a day. Tickets for the short trip are under $5, for the longer trip about $10. For complete schedules and rates at the time you plan to visit, write Rail Tours, Inc., P.O. Box 285, Jim Thorpe, PA 18229 or call (717) 325–4606.

Across the street from the station, you see the **Old Mauch Chunk Scale Model Railroad HO Display** on the second floor of the Hooven Mercantile Co. The display is open from July 4 to October 31, noon to 5:00 P.M. daily and from November to June 30, weekends, noon to 5:00 P.M. A modest admission fee is charged. On the first floor of the mercantile building specialty shops laid out in emporium fashion, without partitions, feature coal jewelry and sculptures, dolls, decorated eggs, and various other craft items and supplies. Call (717) 325–2248 for more details.

From Hazard Square, walk up Broadway to check out the quaint old stores and buildings. The Mauch Chunk 5 & 10 seems much as it must always have been, except for the prices and plastic toys. **The Bookworm,** a relatively new business, combines a bookstore and an ice cream parlor with an old-time soda fountain. The owners, Rick and Hanna Schein, know a lot about Jim Thorpe's changes and restoration and are glad to talk about it. Anne's Early Attic, a funky little shop, buys and sells antiques and collectibles. At Cassie's Restaurant in the New American Hotel, you can enjoy a good meal in the Victorian dining room or on the outdoor upper balcony. It is open seven days a week, 11:00 A.M. to 2:00 A.M..

One block south of Broadway, Race Street, a narrow alley, winds along the path once taken by an old mill race past old buildings and more specialty shops and Stone Row, built by Asa Packer in 1848. Today long-time residents and shopkeepers live side by side with newly arrived artists and writers. If you are or if you know a cat lover, the **Cat's Paw Gallery** (717–325–4041) will be a sure stop. It contains a collection of crafts and fine art in ceramic, metal, wood, glass, and textiles, as well as prints, paintings, and drawings, all inspired by cats and created by well-known northeastern Pennsylvania artists.

Having seen the Stone Row houses built by Asa Packer, you may want to drive up the hill on U.S. Route 209 to tour the **Asa Packer Mansion,** providing a dramatic contrast to the cabins of Eckley Miner's Village at Hazleton. The lavishly decorated Victorian home was built in 1850 by European craftsmen and furnished in mid-nineteenth-century opulence. It stands the same today as it was when the Packers celebrated their fiftieth wedding anniversary—preserved rather than restored. Among the outstanding pieces in the house are the first-prize gas chandelier of the 1876 Centennial Exposition and the crystal chandelier copied for the film *Gone with the Wind.* Along with fine carved walnut furniture and the desk, chair, and bookcase belonging to General Robert E. Lee, you'll find good collections of paintings, sculpture, crystal, and china. Asa Packer is said to have earned all this, working his way from humble beginnings to become the founder and president of Lehigh Valley Railroad, founder of Lehigh University, and a philanthropist on the grand scale. The mansion is open noon to 5:00 P.M. on weekends following Easter and daily beginning Memorial Day weekend until October 31, then closed until the weekend after Easter except for the first week in December, when the museum keeps regular hours. A modest admission fee is charged.

One of Asa's gifts, possibly philanthropic, to his son, Harry, was a brick and stone mansion in the style of the Second Empire, practically next door. This house is lavish, too, with hand-decorated ceilings and Victorian antiques, including some pieces that belonged to the Harry Packer family. The Harry Packer Mansion is open for tours and also operates as a bed-and-breakfast inn, with thirteen rooms, some with private bath, available for guests. A stay includes full breakfast in the morning. The mansion is open for tours Sunday through Friday, noon to 5:00 P.M. The mansion has mystery weekends and also sometimes turns over the entire establishment to wedding parties and special celebrations, so be sure to call before you plan a tour or if you want to spend the night (717–325–8566).

Another bed-and-breakfast inn somewhat away from the bustle of downtown, is the Lausanne House, at 97 West Broadway, a Victorian house where the coffee pot is always on and the cookie jar is always full. You can help yourself anytime. Call (717) 325–8721.

The Poconos

Sometimes you see promotional material saying that Jim Thorpe is in the foothills of the Poconos. In Jim Thorpe, they like to advertise themselves as the Little Switzerland of America. As you climb back up the mountains to leave the town, you see where a town looking for tourists got the idea. Unfortunately for those seeking areas yet unexploited, many parts of the rest of the Poconos already have more tourists than they can fit comfortably into heart-shaped bathtubs and serve with fruity pink cocktails at poolside bars. To see some of the lesser known parts of the Poconos, take Route 209 out of Jim Thorpe toward Lehighton. In its time, Route 209 was a major highway in the state, important enough to displace homes and cemeteries and prize stands of sugar maples in its construction. This route has lost much tourist traffic to interstates; here and there you still see a failed group of tourist cabins predating today's motels or an abandoned gas station with weeds growing through the macadam. These properties might be good investments for people who can afford to wait for a return, because traveling on Interstate 80 has become nearly unacceptable here. Huge repair projects and slow trucks hauling double trailers up the mountains often back traffic up for miles. The highway is in such bad condition physically that it's hard to see how the state will ever catch up. One can imagine traffic returning to Route 209 in sheer desperation. By today's standards it's narrow and slow because of the steep hills and curves, but the surface is in fairly good condition, trucks pull over to let traffic pass, and most of the countryside is lovely. Even where it's not beautiful, it's interesting. This highway skirts Lehighton.

In Lehighton most folks speak in noticeable Pennsylvania Dutch accents; many have lived here all their lives, as have their parents and grandparents and even great-grandparents. **Trainer's Inn,** directly on Route 209 just outside Lehighton, reflects such stability and tradition. The Green family has run Trainer's for nearly forty years, Dick and Linda having only recently turned over operations to their daughter, Linda. Countless weddings, anniversaries, engagements, births, and birthdays have been celebrated with lunch or dinner here. It's as though that spirit gets into the woodwork. Stopping for your own lunch or dinner at Trainer's, you move at warp speed back to a time and place where big families celebrated together, friends saw each other regularly over decades, and the whole crew counted up the new babies every time they got together for a reunion. Even the menus recall those times. Remember platter dinners—roast beef, ham, or capon, with soup or fruit cup, potatoes, two vegetables, dessert, and a relish tray? Trainer's still serves platters at moderate prices. Lunch choices include the standards, club sandwiches, hot sandwiches, soups, salads, burgers, and fries, as well as such specials as fried country sausage, haddock, tenderloin, and a long list of vegetables. Beer, wine, and cocktails are also available. Trainer's is open from 11:30 A.M. to 8:30 P.M. Monday through Thursday, to 10:00 P.M. Friday and Saturday, to 7:00 P.M. Sunday. Call (215) 377–4350.

Continuing a few miles north on Route 209, just before Trachsville, you come to another eating place, one you might zip on by because of its roadstand appearance. Stop. At the **New Apollo Restaurant,** Alexander and Susan Dahab prepare and serve authentic Greek and Middle Eastern food, including spectacular baklava, less sweet and sticky than most, that some customers drive two hours from Philadelphia to buy in quantity. The Dahabs make everything fresh, to order: hummus, fried eggplant with tahini sauce, grape leaves stuffed with ground meat and rice, falafel balls, spanakopita—most of the standard favorites. If you can get here during a slow time, part of the fun is talking to Susan and Alexander, hearing the Horatio Algerish story of how they came from Egypt and Greece to New York City (where Alexander was an artist and photographer and Susan managed their family beauty salon) to retire and run this little roadside restaurant close to their Pocono summer home. Alexander even upholstered the red booth seats himself. But perhaps you need to hurry. If you call ahead or don't mind waiting, they'll prepare anything on the menu for takeout. The New Apollo has attracted Lehighton business people away from the quick-food chains—for some it's now baba ganoush instead of burgers. The restaurant is open Monday through Saturday 11:00 A.M. to 10:00 P.M. and Sunday 1:15 P.M. to 10:00 P.M. Phone (215) 681–5776.

From Lehighton, head north on Route 209 to Kresgeville, where you can stop for a break or (if you haven't already overdone it at Trainer's and The New Apollo) a meal at **The Inn at Kresgeville.** Marylou and Joe Geltz recently restored this Victorian inn, beautifully finishing the floors, putting up lace curtains, and preserving the original pressed-tin ceilings. Not that you stop at such a place to look at floors and ceilings. More to the point, daily luncheon specials such as roast baron of beef and a good selection of dinner steaks and seafood attract tourists and local diners alike. If you're too full already, spend a few minutes having a drink at the old-timey bar listening to the music of people speaking in Pennsylvania Dutch accents. The inn is open daily 11:00 A.M. to 11:00 P.M. and Sunday to 9:00 P.M. Phone (215) 681–6595.

Cherry Valley

Drive on fifteen or so minutes on Route 209, then take Route 33 south at the Saylorsburg exit. Almost immediately, turn left on Old Route 115, Lower Cherry Valley Road, and follow the signs into the **Cherry Valley Vineyards,** a friendly little winery run by Dominick Sorrenti and his family. The setting is entirely rural and the atmosphere in the salesroom casual. Nobody puts on airs here, even though some of the wines are good enough to warrant it. The Sorrentis have produced a limited amount of absolutely wonderful Chardonnay that they themselves dare to describe as "dry, delicate, incredibly wonderful balance." Well, false modesty serves no one. They also produce a genuinely dry champagne and, for those with sweeter tastes, several fruity semi-dry wines that manage a fresh taste of grapes without being foxey or syrupy sweet. Tours include information about the wine's fermentation, filtering process, and bottling. The winery is open daily from 11:00 A.M. to 5:00 P.M.; tours are given Saturday from 11:00 A.M. to 5:00 P.M. and Sunday from noon to 5:00 P.M. Call (717) 992–2255.

A quick jog back on 33 north takes you to Snydersville, which isn't much more than a gas station and a school bus stop, but several antique dealers have opened shops in old homes here. The names and proprietors may change, but this remains a good area for antiquing, where the dealers are knowledgeable but not in the thick of the tourist stream.

At Snydersville you pick up Business 209 (paralleling Route 209) going toward Stroudsburg. The business route is slower but less heavily traveled and more interesting. Before you get to Stroudsburg, take the Shafer Schoolhouse exit and follow the signs to **Quiet Valley Living Historical Farm.** The quality of this site and the passion of the people who make it work defy superlatives. More than twenty-five years ago, Alice and Wendell Wicks, with their daughter and son-in-law, Sue and Gary Oiler, saw the possibilities for this Pennsylvania German farm that dates from 1765. The Wicks and the Oilers poured work and time and money into the project. Researching, repairing, and collecting furnishings and farm equipment, they opened Quiet Valley as a living museum, showing how the original Pennsylvania Dutch family lived on this virtually self-sufficient homestead from 1765 to 1913. For a time, the Oilers actually lived in the top floor of the home. Over the following quarter century, with hens and newly hatched chicks at their feet, and sheep, pigs, and other barnyard animals with their young living on the farm, the two families restored the existing buildings to full function and reconstructed others that would have been there.

Using costumed area residents as role players, Quiet Valley takes you through the daily routines and seasonal activities of the colonial family. One of the most interesting parts of the tour is the earthen-floored cellar kitchen in the main building. At first, the settling family lived entirely in this room, with only the clay hearth fireplace for heat and cooking. A costumed guide uses the cooking utensils and talks about her life as a colonial woman. Outside, the baker offers you samples of applesauce cake or corn bread from the brick oven. Your kids join kids in costume petting the animals and jumping in the hay. Everybody gets a little dirty, a little itchy, and a little sneezy. Quiet Valley differs from most living museums in the uncanny sense of reality it achieves. It's nice to hold on to the feeling awhile after the tour by picnicking in the grove. Quiet Valley is open June 20 to Labor Day, 9:30 A.M. to 5:30 P.M. weekdays and 1:00 P.M. to 5:30 P.M. Sundays. The last tour begins at 4 P.M. A moderate admission fee is charged. Call (717) 992–6161.

Should Quiet Valley set you up for more country life, you might drive to East Stroudsburg and spend the night at The Inn at Meadowbrook, built in 1842. In a country setting of hills and meadows, Meadowbrook offers opportunities for skating, skiing, fishing, swimming, tennis, walking, and reading by the fire, depending on your mood and the season. For full details write the Overmans, R.D. 7, Box 7651, East Stroudsburg, PA 18301 or call (717) 629–0296.

Lower Delaware River Valley

From here you are close to the **Delaware Water Gap.** It is part of a National Recreation Area between New Jersey and the Pocono Plateau in Pennsylvania. Publicity calls it "the eighth wonder of the world." Even in the nineteenth century it attracted the well-to-do for resort holidays away from the heat. The beauty of the gap lies partly in the contrasting colors of layers of quartzite, red sandstone, and dark shale that have been revealed as the river eroded its path ever deeper over geologic eons. One way to see some of this, yet get a break from driving, is to ride the Delaware Water Gap Trolley. Like most development around the Water Gap, the tour is frankly commercial. Guides give a spiel about history, points of interest, settlers, and Indians, but it would be a shame to miss the natural splendor of the gap chewed through the mountains by the Delaware River because of a superficial and not necessarily permanent layer of commercialism. The

Delaware Water Gap

trolley depot is on Route 611 at the center of Delaware Water Gap.

With a little light hiking you can appreciate the gap closer at hand. Park in the Resort Point parking lot off Route 611, on the Pennsylvania side. Across the road, stone steps take you to a trail paralleling a stream that goes up steeply for a short distance, then turns left onto a marked trail. The trail continues gently upward for about a mile, and when you get to a waterfall, you can no longer hear the traffic on Route 611. A little farther straight ahead a large rock outcropping overlooks the entire gap. In this area you can also drive into some overlook points from which you see a spectacular view without hiking. Signs direct you to these. At one such place, a souped-up red Chevrolet once roared in, a couple of teenagers slurping diet Cokes looked out, said, "There isn't anything here," and roared away. It happens regularly. Pushing these people over the edge is against state and national regulations. For full information on the Delaware Water Gap National Recreation Area, write to the offices: Bushkill, PA 18324 or call (717) 588–6637.

In the same area, off Route 209 at Bushkill, **the Mary Stolz Doll and Toy Museum** features about 125 dolls representing cultures from around the world, as well as many miniature rooms Mary has created and an assortment of related old toys. The collection began when Mary started collecting dolls in 1910. Her interest has been continued in the family for four generations. Bill and Jan Stolz own the museum now. Looking without touching in such places isn't too difficult; looking without owning can be sheer torture for a committed collector. The gift shop offers relief in its collection of dolls, teddy bears, doll houses, and miniatures. The museum is open seven days a week; call for hours (717–588–7566).

Directly across from the doll museum, **The Pocono Indian Museum** shows the history of the now-extinct Delaware Indians in six rooms of collected artifacts. Visitors listen to a half-hour tour cassette explaining the displays as they walk through the exhibits. Some of the pottery is more than 1,000 years old. Weapons and tools have had only their handles reconstructed. The Delaware Indians didn't fit the stereotype typified by the drugstore wooden Indian. They wore simple deerskin garments, cut their hair short, and used no feathers, except perhaps a few for ceremonies. Nor did they live in tepees. One room in the museum holds a reconstructed bark house of the kind the Delawares made for themselves by lashing together saplings and covering them with strips of elm or oak bark. Another room in the museum exhibits artifacts from various western Indian tribes, even a 130-year-old scalp. If that seems a little gory, you can cover your eyes as you pass. In the museum gift shop you can buy souvenirs made by surviving Indian groups. Hours are daily, 9:30 A.M. to 6:00 P.M. A modest admission fee is charged. Call (717) 588–9338.

Also on Route 209 at Bushkill, **The Craft Gallery of Pennsylvania Designer Craftsmen** exhibits and sells the work of juried members of the Pennsylvania Guild of Craftsmen: weaving, pottery, gold, silver, brass, pewter, soft sculpture, leather, Scherenschnitte, basketry, and so on. It is open from May 17 to October 26, Wednesday through Sunday from 10:00 A.M. to 5:00 P.M. Call (717) 588–9156.

Land of Many Waterfalls

More glorious than the creations of any human hand, **Bushkill Falls,** known as "The Niagara of Pennsylvania," is easy to reach, 2 miles northwest of U.S. Route 209. Easy walking over rustic bridges and a nature trail of about a mile and a half takes you through virgin forests, past a gorge from where you can view eight waterfalls, the largest of which is Bushkill, dropping 100 feet. These falls have attracted generations of artists and photographers. Even with a simple camera it's possible to make spectacular pictures. You may picnic, boat, and fish in the park. Some food is available. The park is open daily 9:00 A.M. to dusk, April through November. Rates are moderate. Phone (717) 588–6682.

At Dingmans Ferry, farther north on Route 209 but still in the Delaware Water Gap National Recreation Area, Dingmans Falls, the highest waterfall in Pennsylvania, pours down over a hundred feet of rock with awesome power. On the same easy trail, in woods of hemlock and ferns, Silver Thread Falls, not quite as high but equally beautiful, is another stop worth a few photographs. In the park's nature center you can study an audiovisual program or pick up a map and talk to a naturalist about the falls and good trails to walk. You'll find lots of easy trails here, good for those whose fitness falls short of perfection.

Upper Delaware River Valley

From Dingmans Ferry it's only about 10 miles more to Milford, a good place to spend the night—or several nights if you can spare the time. **The Swiss Country Inn,** in an 1800s farmhouse on twenty acres with a creek and pond, has everything you'd need to spend most of forever in comfort. The innkeepers, Klaus and Lyda Buschan, fill the place with fine food and wines, a lounge with a bar and fireplace, good music, and good books. For details write Box 366, Milford, PA 18337 or call (717) 296–6939.

If you can't envision forever without a golf course, try the Cliff Park Inn, completely surrounded by a golf course that has been in operation since 1913. Talk about a mature course! This inn, an 1820 Buchanan farmhouse, has three dining rooms serving food one guest called "a gourmet's dream." She was hooked by the quail stuffed with raisins and apples, flamed in brandy and covered with a truffle sauce. In addition to ten rooms with private bath, the inn rents three cottages. Write the inn at Milford, PA 18337 or call (717) 296–6491.

While you're in Milford, stop at the Upper Mill, a nineteenth-century water-powered mill where water rushing over a three-story-high waterwheel powers the grinding stones and also generates enough electricity to light the mill. The mill is open from April until winter, 9:30 A.M. to 5:30 P.M., with frequent tours and demonstrations. Call for fall and winter schedules. The mill (717–296–6313) is on Sawkill Creek at Water and Mill Streets.

From Milford, driving west on Interstate 84 for about half an hour brings you to another place it would be pleasant to spend several days, the **Sterling Inn,** in South Sterling. It's a sixty-room hostelry on more than a hundred acres, with hiking and cross-country ski trails, a nine-hole putting course, tennis court, and a swimming and skating pond. Four of the new rooms have Franklin stoves. Local cooks prepare American meals—roast beef, chicken, seafood, and fruit and berry pies. Write Sterling Inn at Box 2, South Sterling, PA 18460 or call (717) 676–3311 for rates and reservations.

For a different kind of stay, go northwest from Milford on Route 6 to try **Settler's Inn,** run by Grant and Jeanne Genzlinger. This family-style place furnished in "early attic" and run with lots of help from family and friends, is casual in everything except food, which is definitely full-scale gourmet—baked stuffed shrimp, broiled lamb chops, veal Oscar, pecan torte with strawberry filling—all the foods that you should pat directly on your hips, since that's where they end up anyway. The inn is near Lake Wallenpaupack, where you can fish and boat. For more information about Settlers' Inn write 4 Main Avenue, Hawley, PA 18428, or call (717) 226-2993.

Upper Delaware Wilds

A considerably more rustic alternative to Sterling and Settler's is a country vacation at **Sylvania Tree Farm** on the Delaware River in Mast Hope. Mast Hope is one of those you-can't-get-there-from-here places. From Milford take Route 6 about 14 miles to Route 434, go north about 3 miles to Route 590 west to Lackawaxen, then turn right toward Mast Hope. Ask for a brochure with full directions when you make your reservations. The destination worth the trouble of all these little roads is 1,250 acres on the river shore with woods, fields, brooks, and seclusion. You can stay in a modern cottage or pitch your tent at a campsite. It's a naturalist's paradise. The property is in the Upper Delaware Wild and Scenic River corridor, administered by the National Park Service. Watchful visitors sight bald eagles and blue heron in the valley, and white-tail deer, black bears, beavers, and foxes in the woods and fields. You can cross-country ski in winter, hike other times, and book canoe and rafting trips with nearby outfitters. Also, the National Park Service gives tours of the river valley and several historic sites. Write Sylvania Tree Farm, Box 18, Mast Hope, Lackawaxen PA 18435 or call (717) 685-7001.

Antique Airplane Restaurant

Off the Beaten Path in Southeastern Pennsylvania

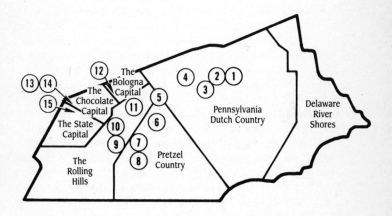

1. Daniel Boone Homestead
2. Antique Airplane Restaurant
3. Shillington Restaurant and Farmers Market
4. Conrad Weiser Homestead
5. Michter's Distillery & Jughouse Outlet
6. General Sutter Inn
7. Sturgis Pretzel House
8. Candy Americana Museum
9. The Winery at Mt. Hope
10. Cameron Estate Inn
11. Cornwall Iron Furnance
12. Weaver's and Baum's Lebanon Bologna
13. Barbara's Mini World
14. Hershey's Chocolate World
15. State Museum of Pennsylvania

Southeastern Pennsylvania

Pennsylvania Dutch Country

In this part of Pennsylvania, paths have been not only beaten, but flailed, paved, and planted with billboards. Unquestionably, the main attraction has been Pennsylvania's Plain People—the Amish. The "fancy" Pennsylvania Dutch of hex signs, *schnitz und knepp*, scrapple, and shoefly pull a close second. The official center of tourist activity, Lancaster and the little towns nearby with racy names like Intercourse, Blue Ball, and Bird-in-Hand, does not appear in this guide because the area is nearly touristed to death. Although more than 16,000 Amish still live here, a steady emigration to escape tourism and to find more farmland for the children in their large families has spread the Amish population through virtually all of Pennsylvania's rural areas. Almost any of them offer an off-the-beaten-path traveler a less frenetic, more tasteful opportunity to learn about the beliefs and customs of the Plain People, or at least of the Amish. Moravians, Mennonites, and Dunkards, also historically part of Pennsylvania's tradition, have escaped the commercial blitz.

As for the Fancy Dutch, those lovers of art and color and music, commercialization makes it hard to sort out the authentic from the bogus. There are just too many cute sayings, too much "home cooking," too many placemats and T-shirts printed with stylized tulips and birds.

The character of the area has changed not only because of tourism but also from increasing population. Rural villages swelled into Reading suburbs. One-room schools in Shingleton, Fleetwood, and Breezey Corner, where kids named Yenser, Schmidt, Dietrick, and Schucker used to leave their shoes outside the schoolhouse doors after they'd been sprayed by skunks caught in their trap lines, now house corporate executives. Expensive shrubs replace the old outhouses. A swimming pool company takes over the abandoned post office building. In place of the worn old realities, recreations and specialty shops scream for tourist dollars.

The burgeoning factory-outlet business has also changed the character of the area. Literally hundreds of outlets, mostly housed in old factory complexes in Reading, attract shoppers by the bus load. Sometimes they stay for a week or longer to work through the outlets looking for bargain prices on brand-name merchandise. Motels and restaurants geared to the bargain-hunting family increase in number yearly. Whatever the value of the phenomenon to local economy, it dilutes the local, homey feel of the area and fills up spots that until recently were still hideaway spots.

But don't yield to the temptation to skip the whole thing and head for uninhabited hills, because at the fringes of official Dutch country you can still find towns where people go about their work much as ever, cook and serve the hearty meat-and-potatoes stuff of their ancestors, and speak about everyday things, without scripted sayings, in the quick cadences of inherited German accents. So chust you vait oncet before you give up. There's good here yet, say not?

Start 9 miles east of Reading on Route 422 in Birdsboro at the **Daniel Boone Homestead.** Judging from the number of Boonetowns, Boonevilles, and Boones in the country, ole Dan'l got around, leaving historic sites behind wherever he stopped. He was born at this homestead to frontier parents in 1730 and raised here among the few English Quaker, German, Swiss, Huguenot, and Swedish pioneers who settled the area. He lived here for sixteen years, raising cattle for his father and getting friendly with the Shawnees, who probably taught him many of the outdoor skills he used the rest of his life. The restoration of the Boone Homestead, which was done mostly between 1940 and 1950, includes the foundation of the original log house and an addition the Boones built of stones, as well as a barn, blacksmith shop, and sawmill. The furniture is not what the Boones had, but the antiques all date from the 1780s and were gathered from the area. Guided tours lasting about forty-five minutes show how the Boones lived and also explain the differing practices of the various other cultures represented in Pennsylvania in the 1700s. The guides go into considerable detail about the history and uses of the furnishings as well. In addition to the buildings, the homestead has 600 acres of fields, woods, and a lake. Walking and biking trails are open from dawn to dusk daily. The area abounds in songbirds, wild flowers, and wildlife, including painted turtles that sun themselves on rocks protruding above the surface of the lake. With a little more exploring you can discover a woodchuck den, parts of a chestnut fence, and trails left by small animals. The homestead is open Tuesday through Saturday, 9:00 A.M. to 5:00 P.M. and Sunday noon to 5:00 P.M. It is closed Monday and holidays, except Memorial Day, July 4, and Labor Day. There is a modest fee for touring historic buildings. Call (215) 582–4900 for more information.

To get back to those human needs that can't be satisfied by history and hiking, if you'd like a novel place to eat where the food is basically Pennsylvania Dutch without being self-conscious about it, stop at Dutch Colony Motor Inn and **Antique Airplane Restaurant** at the East Junction Reading Bypass and Route 422 (4653 Perkiomen Avenue) east of Reading. Suspended from the ceiling, a Monocoupe built in 1927 in Illinois could still fly today if you took it outside and gassed it up. Breity Breithaupt, an aviator for forty years, found the plane in a barn in Maine, restored it, and flew it to many antique airplane shows before hanging it from the ceiling of the restaurant he and his wife own. Apparently the suspension is perfectly safe; the plane has hung there since 1967. Breity has since collected many other aviation antiques and artifacts, all of which are displayed on a second-floor balcony overlooking the restaurant. Large photographs of Charles Lindbergh add another touch of early flight nostalgia. The best thing that could happen while you're eating here is that at least one little kid will scamper into the dining room, look up, stand stock still in wonder, and then start dancing about under the plane, pointing up and marveling aloud. The waitresses enjoy it and sometimes even create reasons for children from the motel lobby to go into the dining room. The association between airplanes and bad food doesn't hold here. The food is good; the soups and bread are homemade. People who live in the vicinity eat here and chat with waitresses they've obviously known a long time. Although tourists stop at this busy place too, it feels like family. Should you decide to spend the night, the rooms are large and attractive, with good, quiet, central heat and air. A heated swimming pool surrounded by a generous lawn helps you unwind. Rates are moderate; call (215) 779–2345.

From here a quick jaunt on Route 724 takes you to Birdsboro, a little town that still runs on steel, iron, paper, and textiles and hasn't a hint of anything designed especially for tourists, except perhaps the crude, hand-lettered sign: BIRDSBORO, ESTABLISHED 1740. POPULATION 3,481. Stay on Route 724 as it runs along the railroad tracks about 10 miles to Shillington, where you'll come directly to the **Shillington Restaurant and Farmers Market** at the corner of Lancaster Avenue and Museum Road. You'd think from its size and activity that everybody in Berks County eats in the restaurant—businessmen, farmers, and travelers. Ted and Edith Ludwig started with a lunch counter in the Shillington farmers market in 1940. Now a brick building large enough to seat up to 750 people at tables, booths, and counters, the restaurant, still in the Ludwig family, takes advantage of being attached to the farmers market (also owned by the Ludwigs), serving fresh local produce at the three salad bars. The food is in the genuine Pennsylvania Dutch tradition: baked chicken corn pie, chicken pot pie, scrapple, grizzled beef, snapper turtle soup, hot bacon dressing, grilled sticky buns, Black Forest cake, shoofly pie—all fresh and home style. Many of the staff have worked there practically forever and consider themselves part of the Ludwig family, so even though the place is big, the tone is local and friendly. It is open seven days a week, 6:00 A.M. to 8:00 P.M. Call (215) 777–1141. The farmers market sells produce, meats, poultry, and baked goods from Berks County and is open Thursday and Friday, 6:00 A.M. to 6:00 P.M.

After you eat and shop, take Museum Road back to Route 422 west, heading toward Womelsdorf and the **Conrad Weiser Homestead,** a National Historic Landmark. Conrad Weiser was a colonist who maintained close contacts with the Indians, respecting especially their search for a higher power or Great Spirit and their belief in law built on basic moral values in their families. Perhaps because the Indians appreciated that his understanding differed from the more common view of them as uneducated savages without a real culture, Weiser became Pennsylvania's foremost Indian negotiator. He made treaties with the Indians and worked as an interpreter and peacemaker during the French and Indian War. His small stone home, a spring house, and his grave stand on what was once frontier in a twenty-six acre park equipped with lovely picnic areas and public rest rooms. The homestead is open Wednesday through Saturday 9:00 A.M. to 5:00 P.M. from noon to 5:00 P.M. Sundays; it is closed holidays except for Memorial Day, July 4, and Labor Day. A modest admission fee is charged (215–589–2934).

As a bit of lagniappe, spend a few minutes admiring the stock of the Fair Nursery and Landscape Company right beside the park, perhaps picking up a healthy rhododendron to take home if you have room in the car.

After touring the Weiser Homestead and maybe picnicking in the park, you might leave Route 422 to make a loop to several interesting spots before returning to Route 422. Follow Route 419 south to Schaefferstown for a visit to **Michter's Distillery & Jughouse Outlet.** It would be a bad idea to blab this around Kentucky or Tennessee, but Michter's is America's oldest operating distillery, established in 1753 and making sour mash about a hundred years before Jack Daniels laid hand on an ear of corn. John Shenk, a Swiss Mennonite, had more corn than he knew what to do with back in 1753, so he started using it to make whiskey on the bank of Snitzel Creek. Eventually the distillery passed from the Shenk family to Abe Bomberger, who kept on making whiskey until Prohibition shut him down. The restored Bomberger Distillery Building looks as it did in the nineteenth century. Inside, the smallest legal distillery in America, which has hand-hammered copper stills and three small cypress fermenter tubs, still makes one barrel of whiskey a day, as it did in colonial times. The modern distillery makes fifty barrels a day, using the old pot-still sour mash method. Also part of the complex, the old Jug House, where farmers came to fill their jugs on market day, now sells various Pennsylvania Dutch jugs and other whiskey decanters. The Jug House is the only distillery store in the United States. Tour guides explain the sour mash process and the role whiskey played in Pennsylvania development—as an item of commerce, not as an intoxicant. The complex is open daily from 10:00 A.M. to 4:30 P.M.; call (717) 949–6521.

In historic Schaefferstown you can look at the early seventeenth- and eighteenth-century buildings. You may be able to arrange for a tour of the 90-acre living farm and American Life Museum by calling John Hickernell (717–949–3795).

For another outdoor stop, go 2 miles east on State Route 897 to the Middle Creek Wildlife Management Area on Hopeland Road. Of the area's 5,000 acres sheltering waterfowl and wildlife, about 2,500 acres are open to the public. The grounds are open dawn to dusk. The visitor center is open March 1 to November 30, Tuesday through Saturday, 9:00 A.M. to 5:00 P.M. and Sunday, noon to 5:00 P.M. It is closed July 4. Call (717) 733–1512.

Pretzel Country

As long as you're this far south, get on Route 501 and head to Lititz. In the center of town, **The General Sutter Inn,** run by Joan and Richard Vetter, has eleven guest rooms and two suites, all with private bath, and a dining room where the menu dares to deviate from standard Pennsylvania Dutch fare to offer delicacies such as an *escalope* of veal sauteed with wine and mushrooms or chicken Dijon with onions. The inn is named for John Augustus Sutter, who threw himself headlong into the gold rush and never got any of the gold. He came to Lititz to recoup and regroup. Moravians built the inn in 1764 and forbade dancing, singing bawdy songs, or cursing inside. It's probably still not a good idea. John Vetter is a minister, and he has a church organ in the lobby. Somebody must think of doing a little dancing, however; the inn has a bar with Saturday night entertainment. Joan furnished the inn's rooms with Victorian beds and dressers and small antique objects. It is open all year; call (717) 626–2115 for details and reservations.

While you're in Lititz, be sure to visit **Sturgis Pretzel House** at 219 East Main Street, the oldest pretzel bakery in America. It's hard to explain what pretzels mean to a Pennsylvania Dutchman, except to say that they don't make them right anywhere outside the state. Julius Sturgis started baking pretzels in 1861, in a bakery that dates back to 1784. This company's got the hang of it by now. Their pretzels are soft, puffy, golden brown, and salted just enough. Connoisseurs like them with mustard. Bakers twist them by hand, which isn't as easy as it looks, as you'll learn when you take advantage of the opportunity to handle a hunk of dough and try it yourself. While you're at the bakery, you'll see the whole pretzel-making process—from getting the notion to bake some to the final cooling. The tour, which takes about twenty-five minutes, begins with a history of the pretzel, moves to the do-it-yourself stage, then takes you to the modern machines used for manufacturing hard pretzels. Sturgis still makes all its soft pretzels by hand, as they did in the 1800s, and bakes them in the original bakery oven. The last tour begins at 4:00 P.M. Hours are Monday through Saturday, 9:00 A.M. to 5:00 P.M., closed January 1, Easter, Thanksgiving, and Christmas. A modest admission fee is charged. Call (717) 626–4354.

Also in Lititz, you might stop at the Wilbur Chocolate Company's **Candy Americana Museum** and Factory Candy Outlet, at 48 North Broad Street. The tour is an entertaining history of American candy making with demonstrations, including chocolate dipping, and displays of antique equipment. You can buy candy at discount prices in an outlet that looks like a country store. Hours are Monday through Saturday, 10:00 A.M. to 5:00 P.M., closed Thanksgiving and Christmas. Call (717) 626–1131 for more information.

The Rolling Hills

Since you're already into forbidden foods, wash your pretzels and candy down with a little wine. From Lititz, take Route 772 west a bit more than 5 miles to Manheim and **The Winery at Mt. Hope** for tipple and turrets. The Victorian mansion caters to tourism, but in an unusual and tasteful way, worth your time for a change of pace. A wealthy ironmaster originally owned the mansion, and he systematically surrounded himself with more and more splendor, from hand-painted 18-foot ceilings to imported crystal chandeliers. Today hostesses costumed in clothing from various periods of the family's reign from the 1800s to the Roaring Twenties lead you through the refurbished rooms, explain what life was like here, and then, in the billiard room, offer you tastings from the Mt. Hope wine cellars. If you like any of the wines you can buy them in the Vintage Wine Shoppe. After the tour, you're free to walk about the estate gardens, filled with shrubs and plant specimens from all over the world. The French hybrid grapes from which Mt. Hope wines are made also grow on mansion grounds. It is open Monday through Saturday, 10:00 A.M. to 6:00 P.M. and Sundays, noon to 6:00 P.M. The mansion (717–665–7021) is north of Manheim on Route 72.

Mountains named for emotions seem to abound in Dutch Country. When you're done at Mt. Hope, Route 772 takes you to Mt. Joy, a pleasant place to spend the night or have a meal at **The Cameron Estate Inn.** Abe and Betty Groff, the innkeepers, are eighth-generation Lancaster County residents who've found a realistic way to keep an elegant inn in the countryside without going glitzy. The setting is so rural that if you fish in the brook on the property and catch trout, the chef will cook them for your dinner. For those made squeamish by taking fish off hooks, Chef also prepares rainbow trout caught by someone else, plus continental versions of chicken with ham or veal. The inn has the requisite parlor fireplace and veranda, once the scene of heavy political discussion, as well as antique four-poster beds, and oriental carpets. Most of the eighteen rooms have private bath and some have fireplaces. The inn is open year-round; call (717) 653–1773.

Backtrack a couple of miles on Route 772 to Route 72 to head north, crossing the turnpike, to stop at Cornwall and inspect the **Cornwall Iron Furnace** that produced cannon for the Revolutionary War. Before the war it produced stoves and farm tools, a classic case of guns or butter. Pennsylvania's iron deposits were the result of the hot water under the earth's surface dissolving the limestone in the rock and leaving the iron oxide as concentrated iron ore. The location of the furnace, in an area rich in iron deposits, limestone, and timber, made Cornwall a highly productive site. The furnace operated from 1742 to 1883, with workers stoking the fire and pouring molten iron around the clock. The mine was worked until 1972. The restored site includes the original furnace stack, blast machinery, open pit mine, ironmaster's mansion, and wagon and smith shops. The charcoal house is a visitor center displaying exhibits about all phases of mining. Hours are Tuesday through Saturday, 9:00 A.M. to 5:00 P.M. and Sunday, noon to 5:00 P.M. A modest admission fee is charged. Call (215) 589–2934.

The Bologna Capital

It's a drive of only a few minutes from Cornwall up Route 72, back to Route 422 and Lebanon, home of Lebanon Bologna. In the 1800s, Pennsylvania German settlers made this sausage, each family concocting its own recipes and mixing in unusual seasonings. Today most of the Lebanon Bologna eaten in the United States comes from the Lebanon Valley. No other bologna tastes remotely like it, nor does it taste quite the same if you eat it in some other state, no matter where it was made. The recipes are still secret, but the four manufacturers, at two locations, invite visitors, offer tours, maintain museum displays, and offer you good prices in salesrooms. From Route 422, the easiest stop is **Weaver's and Baum's Lebanon Bologna,** just off the highway, 1 mile east of Lebanon at 15th Avenue and Weavertown Road. Signs direct you clearly. As you pull into the parking lot at Weaver's and Baum's, you'll see stacks of firewood, notice the aroma of hardwood smoke, and then you'll watch workers hanging bolognas into wood smokehouses by hand, just as they would have done in the 1700s. The faint odor of smoked meats follows you throughout the plant. By the time you leave, you're ready to sink your teeth into a huge bologna sandwich. While you're there, if customers come in asking for "drops," they're asking for seconds, imperfect products that the companies sell at a discount. Drops are nutritionally fine and perfectly safe, they just don't live up to the Baum-Weaver standards for one reason or another. A common problem is that the bologna is softer in the middle than around the edges, which makes it hard to slice. If you're trying Lebanon bologna for the first time, don't mess with drops; pay the full price and learn how it is at its best. This product doesn't have to be refrigerated as long as the package is sealed, so it's okay to carry it in the car. While you're buying bologna, you can pick up a T-shirt with WEAVER'S FAMOUS LEBANON BOLGNA emblazoned across the front. In Pennsylvania, buying and wearing such a T-shirt makes perfectly good sense. Hours are Monday through Saturday, 8:00 A.M. to 4:30 P.M. Call (717) 274–6100.

The Chocolate Capital

You're into fairly heavy traffic now, going into Palmyra on Route 422, which becomes Main Street. At 132 East Main Street, on the left, stopping at **Barbara's Mini World** changes your pace entirely. Barbara, who builds dollhouses in the 1" to 1' scale, often recreating a customer's own home or hideaway in miniature, enjoys wide admiration in the field for the quality of her work. In the shop she sells fine-quality miniatures handmade by craftsmen specializing in scale work. Don't go in looking for some cute little thing that you can pick up for $5.00; you won't find much in that category. However, for $50.00 or less she sells wonderful stained-glass windows by John Anthony Miller, hand-carved country kitchen furniture by Palmer Dugagrty, a Pennsylvania craftsman, and miniature oil paintings by Pennsylvanian Terry Towe. Serious miniaturists and collectors find good pieces here—not a stop for everyone, but a delight if you're involved in the hobby.

Back on Route 422, breathe deep in Palmyra and you're already in Hershey. You'll know even if you don't see a sign, because the entire town smells endlessly like a pot of boiling cocoa. Lest you miss that clue, all the street lights look like tall posts topped with giant Hershey Chocolate kisses wrapped in silver foil. Even the paper tail with the word *Hershey* on it streams properly from the top of the kiss. It's hard to know how much time in Hershey is enough and how much is too much, especially when you consider that the visitor center of **Hershey's Chocolate World** alone attracts more than a million and a half visitors a year. No Pennsylvanian breathes who hasn't heard of Hershey, and few live who haven't visited here at least once in their lives. You may not want to devote days to the attractions, but you should know about the phenomenon. Hershey is clearly a company town, exactly in the manner of a coal town or textile town, albeit more prosperous.

It all started with the Hershey bar. Today Hershey Foods Corporation comprises many other food manufacturing divisions, including one for macaroni products, but chocolate gets all the noncorporate, that is, *tourist,* attention. Hersheypark (717–534–3916), an eighty-seven-acre theme park has nearly fifty rides, including one of the oldest operating carousels in the country, and a zoo. Hershey's Chocolate World, the corporation's visitor center, gives simulated tour rides showing how chocolate is made. In earlier times, visitors toured the actual plant to see the manufacturing process, sampling chocolate milk and pieces of chocolate candy at the end. You can shop and eat in an indoor tropical garden. It is open seven days a week, 9:00 A.M. to 4:45 P.M. (from noon on Sunday January through April) and closed Easter, Thanksgiving, Christmas, and New Year's Day. Admission is free. Call (717) 534–4900. Hershey Gardens gives guided and unguided tours of its three-season, twenty-three-acre botanical gardens. The Gardens are open daily April through December (717–534–3492). Hershey Parkview Golf (717–534–3450), an eighteen-hole golf course, ranks among the top twenty-five public courses in the country according to *Golf Digest.* Hershey Museum of American Life, next to the park entrance, exhibits Pennsylvania Dutch antiques, American Indian artifacts, and memorabilia of founder Milton S. Hershey. Hours are Memorial Day to Labor Day, daily

10:00 A.M. to 6:00 P.M. and until 5:00 P.M. the rest of the year. It is closed Christmas, Thanksgiving, and New Year's Day. A moderate admission fee is charged. Call (717) 534–3439.

The State Capital

When you've used up Hershey, you'll have to decide whether to stop in Harrisburg, the state capital, or just follow Route 322 into south central Pennsylvania, or go north along the Susquehanna River to the center of the state.

Unquestionably, Hershey gets more hype than Harrisburg, even though Harrisburg is older and about ten times bigger. It started as a trading post in 1710 and even today remains a relatively small city with a population of less than 60,000 and a small-town feel. The State Capitol Building is on Capitol Hill. Guided tours are available free Monday through Saturday, 9:00 A.M. to 4:00 P.M. Call (717) 787–6810.

The **State Museum of Pennsylvania,** William Penn Memorial Museum, and Archives Building, on Third Street between North and Forster displays the original charter King Charles II granted to William Penn. Other exhibits cover military history, science, industry, and decorative and fine arts. The complex houses a planetarium. Hours are Tuesday through Saturday, 9:00 A.M. to 5:00 P.M. and Sunday, noon to 5:00 P.M. The museum is closed major holidays, and admission is free. Call 717-787-4978.

Assuming you don't want to spend much time in a city, even a small one, you can get a good sense of what the old Harrisburg society must have been like by driving along the river on Front Street to look at the old mansions. High taxes and maintenance costs have forced families out of most of them, relegating them to offices for various agencies; consequently they're now exquisitely landscaped and maintained.

Eastern Pennsylvania Wineries

Cefalo's Wine Cellars
22 Rutledge Street
Pittstown, PA 18640
(Phone not listed.)

Chaddsford Winery
Rt. #1 P.O. Box 229
Chadds Ford, PA 19317
(215) 388–6221

Cherry Valley Vineyard
R.D. #4 Box 4343
Stroudsburg, PA 18360
(717) 992–2255

Clover Hill Vineyards and Winery
R.D. #2 Box 340
Breinigsville, PA 18031
(215) 398–2468

Conestoga Vineyards, Inc.-Market
23323 Lincoln Highway
East Lancaster, PA 17602
(717) 397–0228

Country Creek Vineyard and Winery
133 Cressman Road
Telford, PA 18969
(215) 723–6516

Fox Meadow Farm
Chester Springs, PA 19425
(215) 827–7898

Franklin Hill Vineyards
R.D. #3 Franklin Hill Road
Bangor, PA 18013
(215) 588–8708

Hunters Valley Winery
R.D. #2 Box 326D
Liverpool, PA 17045
(717) 564–8177

In and Out Winery
258 Durham Road
Newtown, PA 18904
(215) 860–5899

Laurel Winery
20 Landenberg Manor
Landenberg, PA 19350
(Phone not listed.)

Lancaster County Winery
Rawlinsville Road R.D. #1
Willow Street, PA 17584
(717) 464–3555

Mt. Hope Estate & Winery
P.O. Box 685
Cornwall, PA 17016
(717) 665–7021

Naylor Wine Cellars, Inc.
R.D. #3 Box 424
Ebaugh Road
Stewartstown, PA 17363
(717) 993–2431

Nissley Vineyards
R.D. #1
Bainbridge, PA 17502
(717) 426–3514

Peace Valley Winery
P.O. Box 94
Chalfonte, PA 18914
(215) 249–9058

Preate Winery
Rear 859 South Main Street
Old Forge, PA 18518
(717) 457–1555

Sand Castle Winery
River Road (P.O. Box 177)
Erwinna, PA 18920
(215) 294–9181

Skew Vineyards
R.D. #1 Box 66
Zionsville, PA 18092

Stephen Bahn Winery
R.D. #1, Goram Road
Brogue, PA 17309
(717) 927-9051

Trach Cellars
5541 New Street Box 3119
Allentown, PA 18106
(215) 395-3617

Victorian Wine Cellars
2225 Marietta Avenue
Rohrerstown, PA 17603
(717) 295-9463

York Springs Vineyard & Winery
R.D. #1 Box 194
York Springs, PA 17372
(717) 528-8490

Index

Index

Index

Index

Acknowledgments

This book is much better than it might have been because of suggestions and help from a number of old friends, Pennsylvanians all, who made sure I didn't miss good places. Instead of using the usual author's cryptic phrase, "They know who they are," I'll tell you who they are and say, "They know what they did." Thanks to: John Andrews, Peter Burnet, Tig Burnet, Sister Joan Chittister and the Benedictine sisters of Erie, Carole Coyne, Evan Homan, Sarah Homan, Don Hopey, Kerry Lacey, Jane Musala, Sister Maureen Tobin, Dick Trinca, Judy Trinca. I miss you.

About the Author

Sara Pitzer is a North Carolina–based freelance writer. Before she began writing books, she worked as a feature editor and writer for a Pennsylvania newspaper and wrote for magazines. She considers herself, above all, a reporter, and she prides herself on describing what she sees objectively and accurately.

In addition to *Pennsylvania: Off the Beaten Path,* Sara has written *Recommended Country Inns: South, How to Write a Cookbook and Get It Published,* and *Buying and Selling Antiques.*

Sara lives in the country with two dogs, half a dozen cats, and a very patient husband.

"Off the Beaten Path" series

EDITIONS AVAILABLE

Colorado • Florida • Georgia • Illinois • Indiana
Michigan • Minnesota • New Jersey • New York
Northern California • Ohio • Pennsylvania
Southern California • Virginia • Wisconsin

◆

"Recommended Country Inns" series

EDITIONS AVAILABLE

New England • Mid-Atlantic and Chesapeake Region
The South • The Midwest • West Coast
Rocky Mountain Region • Arizona, New Mexico, and Texas

Don't be puzzled about Pennsylvania.

Learn about your state and others with the enjoyable
and educational 100-piece puzzles in the Austin-Peirce
"Puzzlin' State" puzzle series.

The Globe Pequot Press

For a free catalogue or to place an order,
call toll free outside Connecticut 1-800-
243-0495, in Connecticut 1-800-962-0973;
or write The Globe Pequot Press, Box Q,
Chester, CT 06412.